D0051151

LEADERSHIP
IN THE
WESLEYAN
SPIRIT

LEADERSHIP IN THE WESLEYAN SPIRIT

LOVETT H. WEEMS, JR.

ABINGDON PRESS
Nashville

LEADERSHIP IN THE WESLEYAN SPIRIT

Copyright © 1999 by Abingdon Press

This book is printed on elemental-chlorine–free paper.

Library of Congress Cataloging-in-Publication Data

Weems, Lovett H. (Lovett Hayes)
    Leadership in the Wesleyan spirit / Lovett H. Weems, Jr.
      p. cm.
    ISBN 0-687-04692-0 (pbk. : alk. paper)
    1. Christian leadership—Methodist Church. 2. Wesley, John,
1703-1791. I. Title.
BX8349.L43W44 1999
262 ' . 147—dc21   98-48162
                                                            CIP

Scripture quotations, unless otherwise indicated, are from the New Revised Standard Version Bible, copyright © 1989, by the Division of Christian Education of the National Council of the Churches of Christ in the United States of America.

Scripture quotations noted KJV are from the King James Version of the Bible.

Scripture quotations noted NEB are from *The New English Bible.* © The Delegates of the Oxford University Press and The Syndics of the Cambridge University Press 1961, 1970. Reprinted by permission.

99 00 01 02 03 04 05 06 07 08—10 9 8 7 6 5 4 3 2 1

MANUFACTURED IN THE UNITED STATES OF AMERICA

Portions of this book were presented as the

Franklin S. Hickman Lectures
The Divinity School
Duke University
1993

and the

Bishop Nolan B. Harmon Lecture
Candler School of Theology
Emory University
1995

CONTENTS

INTRODUCTION

"Our newest worlds are sometimes in the past." These words marked the beginning of a lecture Jean Miller Schmidt presented at Saint Paul School of Theology. They are appropriate to begin this journey.[1]

What might the work of leadership in the church today learn from the Wesleyan spirit and tradition? How can the Wesleyan spirit enrich the critical task of discovering a vision for ministry?

Renewing a vision requires both continuity and change. The task is not to repeat the past. Rather the need is to locate the genius behind the achievements of the past from which we can learn for our day.

The futile tendency in the church, however, is to repeat the forms from the past long after they have lost their power. The forms of the past are preserved even as virtually everyone has forgotten the original power and values that gave rise to the forms in the first place.

Leander Keck captured the dilemma well in his Lyman Beecher Lectures. The mainline churches, he contends, "act like inheritors of an estate who camped in the yard because they neither knew nor cared how to live in the house."[2]

Our task is not to return to a time long gone. Rather we seek to learn from Wesleyan principles, practices, and passions. These come from the example of John Wesley and also from the Wesleyan movement itself, especially early American Methodism.

This is a limited and modest undertaking, though not simplistic or sentimental. There is no attempt to lift up John Wesley or any other leader as a model for leadership in our day. John Wesley was an effective leader in many ways. He is the founder of the Methodist movement, of which The United Methodist Church is the largest, though by no means the only, denominational expression. Even so, Wesley, like all leaders of movements, can only provide limited leadership wisdom from his personal example alone.

Neither is there a claim that these contributions are unique to the Wesleyan tradition, nor more important than contributions from other traditions. To the extent that there may be distinctive features, they are indeed gifts for the whole church. If other Christians can benefit from such insights, just as Wesleyans from the beginning have drawn from a myriad of traditions, then such mutual influence would be very much in the Wesleyan spirit.

The effort is not to go "back to Wesley" or to imply a narrow denominational approach to leadership. Rather, the attempt, to use Martin Marty's phrase, is one of "selectively retrieving" Wesleyan themes and then seeking to grow into them for our day.[3]

——PART ONE——

PRINCIPLES OF LEADERSHIP
IN THE WESLEYAN SPIRIT

CHAPTER ONE
Begins with People

Leadership in the Wesleyan spirit begins with people. The beginning point for John Wesley was always people and their needs. More than any other value of Wesley's, it was a holistic concern for the children of God that provided the starting point for leadership decisions and actions.

JOHN WESLEY AS "FOLK THEOLOGIAN"

John Wesley has been called a "folk theologian." Many factors contributed to this designation. A primary one was the passion Wesley had for a faith that connects with the actual spiritual and human needs of all people.

Beginning with people was not a common starting point for religious leaders of his day. This difference in Wesley's approach did not go unnoticed. People with little reason or inclination to take the church seriously paid attention to Wesley. The common people—poor people, working people, people outside the church—heard him gladly. They responded with uncommon enthusiasm. The Southern writer Lillian Smith once described Wesley, his brother Charles, and Methodist evangelist George Whitefield as men "burning with a powerful belief in the importance of the common man's uncommon soul."[1]

In many ways, Wesley was among the least likely of his day to be God's instrument to reach those considered outcasts. His education, background, and personality all might have disqualified him for this missional assignment. Despite all these factors, Wesley connected with people very different from himself. Many previously unreached people came to know the love of Christ because of him. They saw in Wesley a faithful servant of God who cared for them. He cared enough to view ministry through their eyes.

The content of the Wesleyan message was important. But alone it was not enough. Something more was necessary if people previously unreached by the church were to give the message a hearing in the first place. Wesley communicated a care for people. He began with people and their needs. His theology was always a theology for people.

Doctrine was for Wesley a means of connecting God's love, wisdom, power, and redemption to people at their points of need. People never became objects of doctrine, existing only to affirm doctrine for its own sake. People were not in the service of theology. Theology was in the service of the children of God.

PREACHING AS AN EXAMPLE

Wesley's preaching provides one of the clearest illustrations of this principle of Wesleyan leadership. Wesley's texts and sermons varied, often dramatically, from place to place. The reason was that he saw preaching as something that addressed the needs of people with the Word of God. Preaching was never merely the declaration of a fixed "true doctrine" that seeks the assent of hearers.

Wesley's starting point for preaching was people and their needs. He did not go apart, determine what was true theology, and then come back and deliver it as a body of information, waiting for people to say, "Yes, I accept it. Yes,

I agree." Instead, after working very hard to know the breadth and depth of true doctrine, he took as the starting point of each sermon the needs of people in each congregation or gathering.

He drew from the richness of the gospel just the word most essential to connect the needs of the people with the love of God. That was not the total word, it was not the last word, but it was the beginning word for people.

So when Wesley was with people who were "down and out" with little regard for themselves, as in Newcastle or Billingsgate, he delivered a word of forgiveness, grace, and love. On the other hand, if he was with people who were wealthier and self-satisfied, such as a congregation in Clifton, he drew from another word to puncture their self-righteousness. In every case he began with people and their needs.

Wesley defied a church callous to common people, declaring he would preach nothing but "plain truth for plain people." Although concerned about theology, Wesleyans had as their main interest that every person experience God in a profound way. To do this they needed an "idiom in touch with people."[2]

RESPECT FOR THE LISTENER

Wesley's profound care and respect for listeners made it possible for him to be an effective preacher without extraordinary oratorical skills. Often thousands listened intently to his sermons. A historian relying on eyewitness evidence describes Wesley's speaking in public as "chaste and solemn" and not marked by the eloquence of a preacher such as George Whitefield. There was in Wesley's preaching a "divine simplicity . . . in his manner which commanded attention."[3]

A present-day writer on preaching advocates "courteous speech" in preaching. Courteous speech is respectful of the listener. It respects the autonomy of the hearer. Courteous speech is the opposite of coercion. What would it mean, asks Barbara Brown Taylor, to practice "chastity in our preaching"—to make modest proposals in the simplest language available, to trust the influence of unsullied speech?[4] Wesley's preaching did so and, in manner and content, treated listeners with respect as children of God.

THE DEMOCRATIZATION OF AMERICAN CHRISTIANITY

In America we see the powerful example of this Wesleyan priority for people. Historian William Warren Sweet points to the Methodist concern "to win people of all kinds." Some denominations sought out communities on the frontier that shared their backgrounds and ancestry. The Methodists, on the other hand, saw their ministry as being not to any one class or group but thought in terms of all the people making up the rapidly expanding western society.[5]

Nathan Hatch identifies the "genius" of American evangelicals in the eighteenth century as their "firm identification with people." He points to the many ways that Wesleyan leadership contributed to the "democratization of American Christianity." Others focused on "articulating and defending the truth and building great institutions." Evangelicals, such as the Methodists, put their passion into communicating the gospel message. They proclaimed the good news simply and clearly to all kinds of people.[6]

NO STERILE VIRTUES

It quickly becomes clear that leadership in the Wesleyan spirit goes well beyond true ideas and pure values.

Mary Parker Follett, an early-twentieth-century writer on organizational life, maintained that personal honesty exhausts no one's duty in life. Instead, an "effective life" is demanded of us. No "isolated honesty" gives us social effectiveness. "When we go up to the gates of another world," she says, and "there announce, 'I have been honest, I have been pure, I have been diligent,'—no guardian of those heavenly gates will fling them open for us." Instead, we shall hear, "How have you used those qualities for making blossom the earth which was your inheritance? We want no sterile virtues here. Have you sold your inheritance for the pottage of personal purity, personal honesty, personal growth?"[7]

Effective leadership begins not with some fixed ideology—although one's values always will be integral to leadership. Leadership begins with people.

I remember my surprise in the 1960s when I read sermons Martin Luther King, Jr., had preached as pastor of Dexter Avenue Baptist Church in Montgomery, Alabama, a few years before. What surprised me was not the content of the sermons, but that he used for his scripture readings the King James Version of the Bible.

One has to remember that it was in an era when nearly all "educated" clergy were steadfastly reading from the Revised Standard Version (RSV). Not only was the RSV a fine translation for that time, it was also under tremendous opposition from fundamentalists. Refusing to read from the King James Version was almost an article of faith for literate clergy I knew in that polarized situation. King's reading from the King James Version helped me understand that he was a pastor who understood there were more important issues for him to face at the time. It also showed me a pastor more concerned with effective ministry in a particular congregation than with what others might think of him. He began with his people.

This Wesleyan dimension of leadership can save us from a theology that sets up shop for itself and is unrelated and unresponsive to people and their needs. It can warn us about an approach to preaching that gives generous attention to content and little regard to how people experience, or even hear, the message. It can help us avoid a leadership based more on the leader's goals and values than on the actual needs in a particular time and place crying for faithful attention.

"PEOPLE GOD HAS GIVEN US"

This Wesleyan model should also guard us against the preoccupation of many leaders today with self as the beginning point for leadership. The beginning point for leadership is not "my style, my story, my vision, my needs, my values." The beginning point for the ministry of leadership in the Wesleyan spirit is the "people God has given us," to use Martin Niemöller's phrase, and the gospel that we believe brings new creation.

A pastor in a denominational extension ministry told a colleague about the three churches of her denomination where she lived. She said that at one church everything is "high and lifted up" with great preaching and great music. At another church it is one big family. Then at the third church it is hard to figure out what is happening! Her colleague's response was, "In the course of your ministry you may be pastor of all three of those churches." This pastor must develop leadership skills to minister effectively in a variety of churches just as different from one another as these three.

When leadership begins with oneself, very little changes from one leadership role to another. When leadership begins with people and the context of leadership, many things change from one leadership role to another. One can follow some preachers through thirty years of ministry, and not one thing ever changes; not even the spacing or asterisks in the bulletin will change. Over thirty years the whole world has changed. They have not changed because the beginning point for ministry was "my values and my ideas" instead of the beginning point being the context, the people that God has given us. When the context is the beginning point, ministry evolves in much more changing, exciting, and dynamic ways.

FOLK LEADERS

Leaders in the Wesleyan spirit are folk leaders. Such leaders begin with people and their needs because they genuinely love the people.

When I was a pastor, I knew a group of people in the community who shared a vision for a more faithful church and a more inclusive and just community. The thought they had given these issues was impressive. Their ideas about change made perfect sense. A pastor's life can sometimes be lonely, especially when contested issues are at stake. In such times, it is reassuring to find at least a few who share your hopes and dreams, as these people did.

Unfortunately, over and over I saw that these persons were not present when the struggles growing out of their beliefs called for action. When I expressed concern once about their absence, a mutual friend responded with the devastating but apt words, "They love the issues more than the people."

Today, while liberals and conservatives are fighting battles in their "culture wars," many seem to be more in love with the issues than the people. The debate and energy surrounding church and public squabbles among religious leaders mask the shocking and expanding gap between the church and most people. Each church, denomination, and theology has a following, but where is there the passionate concern for all people—especially beyond those naturally drawn to our version of the message?

Spiritual Malaise and Fiscal Woe

Robert Wuthnow captures the result of this dilemma for contemporary churches in describing the "fiscal woes" so many face today. He finds this financial struggle across denominations and churches. But what appears to be a financial challenge is a symptom of a more basic spiritual crisis. The title of his book names the issue as he sees it—*The Crisis in the Churches: Spiritual Malaise, Fiscal Woe.*

Wuthnow finds much of the spiritual crisis to be in leaders who do not understand and identify with the struggles of people with whom they are ministering in their local churches. Many leaders committed to justice efforts find that their efforts succeed best when parishioners' own stifled spirits are liberated, freeing them for an active engagement with the needs of others. A marginalization of parishioners' own hurts simply widens existing divisions. As long as church members must go elsewhere for their own nurture and renewal, the church will never be in a position to challenge them.

So, for Wuthnow, the material problems of churches lie "less in parishioners' pocketbooks than in their hearts and less in churches' budgets than in clergy's understanding of the needs and desires of their members' lives."[8]

Kirk Hadaway and David Roozen describe a Protestant mainstream out of touch. The concerns of millions of ordinary Americans are not uppermost. Many of the "people of all kinds" these churches once reached are no longer present. Many of the people who represented the heart and soul of the Wesleyan faith movement are no longer in the churches. These are the people who, as they put it, are "among us, but not with us."[9]

Faithful and effective Wesleyan leadership begins with people—the people God has given us.

CHAPTER TWO
Follows the People

Leadership in the Wesleyan spirit follows the people so that there will be ministry where the people are.

"FOLLOW THE PEOPLE"

During the Watergate political scandal investigation, a mysterious secret informant known as "Deep Throat" advised journalists Carl Bernstein and Bob Woodward to "follow the money." That concept today often describes a way of getting to the heart of governmental investigations. While "following the money" can be a temptation for churches, leaders in the Wesleyan spirit would do well to observe the early theme of "following the people."

Early American Methodists could have stayed in the cities. That is where the Congregational clergy and others remained. Many factors supported that decision. That is where the most people were. But things were changing. Francis Asbury and others feared that Methodists would remain in the relative comfort of the cities. The need was to follow the people as they moved into the less familiar and more difficult lands to the West to populate what was for them a new nation.

A RURAL STRATEGY

Instead of staying in the cities where the people had traditionally lived, the Methodists chose to go to where the people were moving. As historian Nathan Hatch points out, Asbury developed "a distinct rural orientation adept at expanding into thinly populated areas" as the country was expanding.[1]

Thus, a "sent" ministry followed the movement of the people. Asbury believed such a plan was essential to bringing the gospel to the unchurched in the rural areas. Early American Methodists stretched the concept of "parish." Instead of narrowly circumscribed geographical boundaries, "parish" now became "how far a man and his horse could travel in a year."[2]

Many miss the important lesson from this early history. In discussions about such a sent ministry, the focus is often on who makes appointments and what is "appropriate" consultation. These are important and necessary questions. Yet their resolution is possible without necessarily being faithful to the original missional spirit that gave rise to this form of organizing for ministry. The key lesson is the *purpose* of the sending—to go where the people were going to minister in the name of Christ.

Hatch points out that, in addition to the "traveling preacher," another key to Methodism's early success in America was "its accordionlike power of expansion into every corner of the country." Asbury determined to go where the people were going. "Asbury's mapping of circuits," according to Hatch, "seemed to reflect potential rather than actual membership."[3] All were God's children in need of a ministry of love, salvation, and service.

This missional strategy worked. The system matched the contemporary situation. The results are indeed impressive. Over the next decades Methodism provided perhaps the greatest example of church growth within such a time frame in American history. In a remarkable display of vision, courage, and sacrifice, these leaders in the Wesleyan spirit led a movement that reached virtually every corner of the nation. Methodism, in addition to becoming larger than other churches, became the first denomination represented in every part of the country.

What else would one expect? All the components were there to produce these results. Leaders displayed the utmost dedication to Christ. Their motivation was the conviction that their message was of eternal consequence. They shared Wesley's passion for people. Moreover, they had a plan that put them where the people were.

More at Home in the Country

So we find in early American Methodism a positive rural strategy based on the shifting population realities of the time. There appears also to be another component to this more rural focus that, at least at the time, served them well. Methodists seemed more at home in rural settings. They apparently were more successful in such areas.

An urban presence and vitality were there from the beginning of the Wesleyan movement in America. American Methodists knew well the urban example from their English heritage. Yet, there are a number of indications that Methodists had some uncertainty about city life and their efforts there.[4]

Some Conference histories are illustrative of this attitude. The Delmarva Peninsula (parts of Delaware, Maryland, and Virginia) is one of the oldest and strongest areas of Wesleyan presence and influence in the country. Many different denominational and historical traditions that emerged out of the Wesleyan witness had a presence in this region.

Many of their communities continue to exemplify this history graphically within the United Methodist Church. It is not uncommon today to find several United Methodist churches located very near one another. What makes little sense to the casual observer is understandable to a student of history. Virtually every historical tradition now represented in the United Methodist Church was once strong in this region.

Historian William Henry Williams documented the early Methodist days there. Methodism received its greatest support in the countryside. As in other parts of the country, it was the itinerant system advocated by Asbury that made such a strong and growing rural presence possible. The Delmarva Peninsula had the overwhelmingly rural character of the entire nation.

The location of chapels reflected Methodism's rural strength in the peninsula. In 1784 eighteen of twenty chapels were in the countryside. Chestertown and Dover had the only in-town chapels, and even in Dover the chapel was "somewhat out-of-town." Many well-established communities did not construct Methodist meetinghouses until well into the nineteenth century. Williams says that Peninsula Methodism was "a bit suspicious of town and town dwellers." Many Methodists viewed the larger towns as alien to Methodist values and "famous for wickedness."[5]

As Methodism moved West, the same pattern seemed to follow. A writer in 1843 noted that Methodists did not form classes in the Western (considered Midwest today) towns until years after they had been flourishing in the surrounding settlements. "In this Western work," he noted, "the towns were almost universally avoided by our preachers, as places of too much dissipation for the Gospel to obtain a foothold."[6] In Missouri, for example, only two moderate-sized communities were the exception to this rule.

THE POPULATION BEGINS TO SHIFT

What was the result of this strategy? The numerical success is obvious. Yet, as is often the case, the very success contains within it the seeds of future challenge. It should not come as a surprise that Methodism reached its high point in America at the height of its rural expansion. In terms of membership as a percentage of population, churches that today make up the United Methodist Church reached their high point in 1925 (6.46%).[7] Three-fourths of the people lived in rural areas in 1925.

The population was to shift as much after 1925 as it had previously when pioneers moved west. Doris Kearns Goodwin points out that as late as 1940 America was "a predominantly small-town nation, with the majority of citizens living in towns of fewer than twenty-five thousand people." By the end of World War II, and very much because of the war, "the small-town America . . . had passed into history." More than 20% of the population had relocated during the war years. In addition to military relocation, people "had moved from the farm to the factory, from the South to the North, from the East to the exploding states of the Western rim. . . . The habit of mobility, which would prove both liberating and fragmenting, had become ingrained," she says. "America had become irrevocably an urban nation."[8]

Thus the situation today is just the opposite of the time when Methodism was making its great inroads. Today three-fourths of Americans live in nonrural areas. One-fourth live in cities and one-half live in suburbs.

The most recent census of the United States indicated that 90% of the population growth that took place over the previous decade came in metropolitan areas with a population of one million or more. Half of Americans live today in the thirty-nine metropolitan areas of one million or more people. Three-fourths live in urban places that cover only 2.5% of the land.[9]

EMERGENCE OF "CITY-STATES"

After his study of the last census, Sam Roberts of the *New York Times* said that states are a "political contrivance of cartographers." Today, according to Roberts, the more apt description of the United States is a collection of "city-states" in which three-quarters of the people live around metropolitan areas.[10]

A number of thoughtful researchers and observers see the twenty-first century organized around expansive metropolitan urban areas. Many see this pattern in other countries of the world. Shifting power from the national government to state governments has been a topic of much discussion in the United States. All these discussions today may mean little if populations continue to organize themselves around cities with little regard to state, and sometimes national, boundaries.

"In antiquity," Barbara Crossette reminds us, "there were city-states whose names identified a civilization." For inhabitants, these city-states defined identity and social location to a great extent. These new "megalopolises" are not the city-states of old. The emerging city-states are much more sprawling and diverse. Richard Sennett calls them "cities without a center or an edge." Regardless of size, they are drifting away from national and state identities. They are developing their own political, economic, and occasionally diplomatic identities.[11]

WHERE THE PEOPLE USED TO BE

What does all this mean for leaders today? For United Methodists it means that most United Methodist churches are, for the most part, closer to where the people lived in the 1920s than where they are today. Several denominational studies have compared the location of population and the location of their churches. In one state that is fairly typical of many, this exercise showed 70% of United Methodist churches located where only 30% of the population now lives.

The dramatic impact of this dichotomy between where United Methodist presence is and where the people are is heightened by Jon Margolis's observation that the "frontier is coming back." Margolis notes that in early America, an area could move out of the "frontier" designation when it had a population concentration of at least six persons per square mile. Using the frontier designation of population density (fewer than six persons per square mile), Margolis identifies five Great Plains states where there are more counties now that are "frontier" than in 1920. Thus the phrase "the frontier is coming back."[12]

A CASE STUDY

Kansas presents a good example of the dilemma of demographics United Methodism faces as we move from one century to another.

This state has traditionally been one of the most Methodist states in the country. For this reason it presents a graphic opportunity to trace the success of an earlier strategy of following people as they settled the countryside. It also depicts the failure of later efforts to stay focused on the people as the population became more concentrated as it grew.

The impressive spread and impact of Methodism in Kansas resulted in its becoming the largest denomination there. In the 1950s, for example, the churches that today make up the United Methodist Church constituted the largest Protestant population in 97 of the 105 counties of the state.

What is happening today in this state? Today counties with fewer than six people per square mile ("frontier territory") account for more of the land than they did in 1890.[13] What does this mean for the church? One would assume that the church must be losing members. The church *is* losing membership, but the population is growing and has been for years. What is happening in Kansas is not a loss of people. Instead, population is shifting, not unlike the early days of America, except the movement is in another direction.

One county in the state makes the point replicated across the country in the latter half of this century. This county is on the eastern border of the state and adjacent to a city. Today, census figures indicate that out of 105 counties, this one county has 15% of the population. Since 1990 half the state's population growth has come in this county. The population grew by 600% since 1950. Projections from a regional planning group show growth by another 50% in the next twenty-five years.

Yet, despite this tremendous shifting of population, only 2.5% of the United Methodist churches in Kansas are here.

It would be a mistake to assume that this graphic description of the shifting American population represents only one region. These examples are not out of character with the national patterns that affect virtually every region.

While properly focusing on the places of lost population, the church has not paid appropriate attention to where the people have gone. For a tradition that begins ministry with the needs of people, it is imperative to know where they are and to move with them without forsaking the areas of declining population. That was the early Methodist pattern.

Following the people in those earlier times did not mean abandoning the people of the cities. However, leadership helped define the reality of what was happening so that fitting and appropriate missional responses took place. Their effort was not perfect, but their mistakes occurred in the direction of trying to stay with and serve the people.

WHERE THE PEOPLE ARE TODAY

Urban. Despite the urbanization of America, many large cities have smaller populations today than a half century ago. Eighteen of the twenty-five largest U.S. cities in 1950 had lost population by 1990. One city lost half its population. Cities still are home to 25% of the population. On the other hand, roughly 43% of the poor live in cities today, up from 27% at midcentury.[14]

Suburban. As many large cities lost population in recent decades, seventy-five million people became suburbanites. Today the suburbs are home to the single largest population base. The automobile, along with road construction after World War II, made the suburbs as we know them possible.

Sprawl. A city lost half its population in the last forty years while the surrounding area grew in population. Today, the same number of people live on 30% more land. This phenomenon of outward movement of people includes the suburbs but even more. Some use the word "sprawl" to describe this continuing expansion of metropolitan areas geographically. A whole series of "edge cities" has developed around the periphery of most large cities.

Rural. A nation that was 75% rural at one time is today 75% nonrural. The overall trend of population gravitation toward metropolitan areas continues. Yet in the midst of this overall pattern, there is another movement toward smaller communities and rural areas. "From 1990 through 1995 rural counties had a net influx of more than 1.6 million people, virtually all of it from domestic migration."[15] This is an important trend today, if kept in perspective with other trends.

FOLLOWING WITHOUT ABANDONING

Following the people does not mean following some people and abandoning others. Asbury's rural strategy did not end an urban ministry. He simply recognized a reality. If the Wesleyan message was to have an impact upon people, staying in the cities alone was not enough—but that did not mean the ministry could not stay at all. Likewise, adapting to the shifting populations of today does not mean abandoning areas where people concentrated in Asbury's day.

The last thing needed is a win/lose game. Unfortunately, many church discussions take on this character. A focus on new congregations in growing suburban areas is looked at questioningly by some struggling central-city churches and small-membership rural churches. Expending resources for a revitalized urban strategy does not make sense to some suburban congregations and rural churches. An engaging town and country ministry targeting hundreds of small-membership rural churches appears illogical to some in large membership churches that may have more members than almost all the smaller congregations put together. Sometimes constituencies contend against each other for limited resources. Self-interest is particularly hard to resist in times of decline.

The appropriate question is not about who will be favored or privileged. The essential concern should be the requirements to reach people, minister to them, and engage

them together in ministry beyond themselves. The task is
not a marketing task. It is not a population niche issue. The
motivation is nothing more or less than spreading scriptural
holiness and reform of the nation. It is not possible to do
this effectively without being present in a meaningful way
where the people are—all the people.

Then those in large suburban congregations become passionately interested in the fate of rural congregations
because these churches have a calling essential to an effective Wesleyan witness. Central-city churches will be eager
to make sure that there is an aggressive new-congregation
strategy for urban and suburban areas where appropriate.
They know that the whole Wesleyan witness begins to suffer if churches do not follow the people. Rural churches
will follow with prayerful interest the renewal of central-
city churches, knowing that a movement that abandons
those in the cities can hardly be Wesleyan.

THE CHALLENGE

There is a sense in which the challenges facing heirs of
the Wesleyan movement in America are similar to the challenges facing the nation itself. The Methodist movements in
America and the country itself grew up together. Each
reached prominence in another era. It was a simpler, more
rural America.

Like Methodism, the United States has always had mixed
feelings about cities. Until one person–one vote reapportion-
ment of legislative bodies took place, many politicians rose
to power condemning the cities. Some still do. From Thomas
Jefferson to William Jennings Bryan, claims Joel Kotkin, "anti-
urbanism" has been a part of the American mind-set.[16]

The results of such an attitude are apparent today. Cities
represent what John Gardner calls the "weak link" in gov-

ernment. National and state governments are farther away from the problems and have more money. Cities face the problems directly every day without adequate funds. They do not have the broad tax base of the state, nor the ability of the federal government to print money. Some would say that this description fits many mainline churches located in large central cities.

If the cities present a challenge for the church, so do the suburbs and beyond. Journalist David Broder contends that the "gap between cities and suburbs is probably the biggest challenge to the long-term health of American society." The subject is an "all-but-unmentionable" issue among politicians.[17] It must not be so for the churches.

Churches can take the lead in helping interpret the interrelatedness of everyone's future. The short-term future may seem prosperous for suburbs, exurbs, and some rural areas as people and jobs move in their directions. However, as one suburban mayor put it recently, the long-term health of any region depends on the economic, social, and spiritual health of central cities. Her plea was not to abandon the cities. It is hard to imagine economies, social institutions, or churches remaining vital in today's world without all segments of the nation being strong and connected.

Most problems do not recognize neat boundaries. Almost all problems that affect lives and communities are interrelated. Yet there is very little communication and collaboration across the boundaries. Isolated solutions will not settle interrelated problems.

A PASSION FOR PEOPLE

The Wesleyan movement became a powerful spiritual force in America by going where the people were. The movement did not exist to serve churches. There actually were few churches for many years. The movement did not exist to serve the ordained; there were only a handful anyway. It was a passion and urgency for all to know God's love revealed in Jesus Christ that propelled this movement of God, against all odds, to every corner of a vast nation.

Even as Isaiah answered the call of God saying, "Here am I; send me!" so early American Methodists responded to God's call to be sent. We need to remember the rest of the Isaiah story. Isaiah asked God, "How long, O Lord?" The response to Isaiah reminds us that the call to take God's message of love to all people and places knows no end. Isaiah was called to be faithful

> "Until cities lie waste
> without inhabitant,
> and houses without people,
>   and the land is utterly desolate;
> until the LORD sends everyone far away,
>   and vast is the emptiness in the midst of the land."
> (Isaiah 6:11-12)

CHAPTER THREE
Focuses on Serving

FINDING GOD BETWEEN PEOPLE

The setting for William Golding's novel *The Spire* is a fourteenth-century English cathedral town. The dean of the cathedral, Dean Jocelin, has a dream of doing a wonderful thing for God. He sets out to build a four-hundred-foot spire on the cathedral church as a testimony to the greatness and grandeur of God. Surely if he and the congregation can do this great thing, they will serve God well.

Problems emerge from the beginning. God apparently revealed this vision to Dean Jocelin alone. The congregation does not share the vision. For that reason the congregation becomes divided. Furthermore, the building will not structurally support such a spire. The builder takes on this project after threats and intimidation. The unwise construction jeopardizes his professional reputation. The construction disrupts the services of the church. Workers die in construction accidents. The pastor takes tainted money to keep the project going. The builder becomes involved with the caretaker's wife. She dies in childbirth having his child.

Through everything, Dean Jocelin persists. After all, he is doing a great thing for God. As the novel unfolds, one sees a spire going steadily upward. At the same time there is human suffering and death caused by the project piling up beneath it. Fulfilling this great dream of Dean Jocelin proves to be extremely costly. It is as if Dean Jocelin cannot see what others are seeing, cannot hear what others are hearing, cannot feel what others are feeling. It is as if his religious dream has closed his heart to all other competing values.

Finally, Dean Jocelin no longer can remain oblivious to what is happening around him. He comes to himself, realizes what has happened, and says with sadness, "If I could go back, I would take God as lying between people and to be found there."[1]

Leadership in the Wesleyan spirit begins precisely at that point. It begins with the needs of people and then focuses on meeting those needs through serving in the name of Christ. This involves meeting their personal, spiritual, and material needs. It also means contributing to the larger society as a natural outgrowth of that personal concern. A Wesleyan vision has a more profound impact upon the souls and bodies of people than a four-hundred-foot spire ever can. The story of the Wesleyan movement is indeed one of finding God lying between people and serving God there.

A book on evangelism in the African American tradition describes well this movement that we find in the Wesleyan pattern. The example of Harriet Tubman reflects the Wesleyan combination and sequence. "It was out of this spiritual freedom," the author maintains, "that she decided to move toward her material, economic, and social freedom. . . . It was at the moment of her spiritual liberation that she realized that social liberation from slavery was possible."[2]

SERVANTS OF GOD

The concept of "servant" has a rich biblical tradition. The image of servant is a significant one in the writings of

Isaiah, and in the New Testament the passages are numerous, such as "The greatest among you will be your servant" (Matthew 23:11) and "the Son of Man came not to be served but to serve" (Matthew 20:28). Then there are the questions asked at the judgment of the nations (Matthew 25:31-46), questions which imply the role of servant. Did you feed the hungry? Did you give a cup of water to the thirsty? Did you give clothes to the naked? Did you go to a local jail and minister there?

There are problems with servant language. Almost no English word is sufficient to capture the richness of the biblical meaning. Many words that we use have negative connotations coming out of our own cultural situation, and it is particularly true in this case. Servanthood means subservience for many people. Most of us do not want to be servants, and we do not want to have servants. Despite all these factors, as Maria Harris points out, the concept of servanthood "remains critical in the life of the church and a constitutive part of the Gospel."[3]

Letty Russell acknowledges the problems presented by the concept of servanthood for women and other oppressed groups who have played a servant role not of their own choosing. She speaks of "sisterhood on the way to servanthood," understanding that it is out of strength and identity that one is able to choose servanthood. She can then say that the "role of servant in both the Old and New Testaments is not an indication of inferiority or subordination" and that "regardless of what the role of servant has come to mean in the history of church and society, in the Bible it is clearly a role of honor and responsibility. . . ." She concludes this section by saying that "servanthood is beautiful and powerful for those who accept both its risk and cost!"[4]

Negative images of servanthood are not new. Some of the negative aspects of this imagery were also present in

Jesus' time. He was surely aware of such conditions. The servant language was present in Hebrew scripture, so when Jesus used this language he made clear that he was drawing language from a hierarchical social order. Those who heard Jesus understood that association also. It is as if Jesus was doing what he so often did; he was taking "conventional" language and wisdom and "turning it upside down." When people heard this language, they knew he was taking something considered lowly and declaring it important. He was declaring the reversal of the conventional standards of the world.[5]

WESLEYAN EXAMPLE

Despite shortcomings and limitations, the Wesleyan movement did produce social reform and service of massive proportions. The spirit of revival sparked fires of change never predicted, nor condoned in some cases, by Wesley. Methodist men and women provided leadership for a long succession of social reforms, including the trade union movement, prison reform, and the abolition of slavery.

Albert Outler describes evangelism in the Wesleyan spirit as Wesley teaching his followers to be a "band of martyrs and servants," emptying themselves as servants, giving themselves freely for others. For the early Methodist movement there was a close connection between what happened in the pew and what happened in the jails. What happened in the class meetings connected directly with what happened in the homes of the widows and orphans. It was this "visible martyrdom and servanthood," says Outler, "that rammed home the *evangelion* he preached." Outler reminds us that in the Wesleyan spirit, evangelism and social action are inextricably joined. "The world hears the Gospel when it sees it," he says, "when its witnesses are clearly committed to a more fully human future, in this world and the next."[6]

THRIVING THROUGH SERVING

A lesson for leadership in the Wesleyan tradition is "If you want to thrive, serve." Unfortunately, the message that often comes through in the church is not one of serving those most in need, but asking people to maintain the church. This is especially true during the raising of budgets. The message that comes through indirectly, and sometimes fairly directly, to those in the pews is often "to do something for the church." That same kind of message often comes from beyond the local church level as well. What a strange message this is to communicate. No one ever established a church or denominational unit as objects to be served. Forgetting our original callings can easily happen under the pressure to survive. The message every part of the church is called to proclaim is, "We exist to serve you. And we exist to give you an opportunity together in the name of Christ to meet the needs of a hurting world." If you want to thrive, serve.

It is instructive to observe the differences among church newsletters. Sometimes I ask seminary students to analyze dozens of newsletters. Struggling churches focus on the ordinary (meetings, news of interest only to those most involved) and on obligations, especially financial. Vital churches emphasize what God is doing in people's lives. Primary attention goes to entry points for faith, opportunities for growth in discipleship, the outreach of the church, and especially members' personal involvement.

Don Haynes, a pastor in North Carolina, once asked a tough question. "If your church closed today," he asked, "would anyone miss it other than the members of the church?" Think about that question for a moment. Make a list of the people and groups in your community outside your membership who would miss your church. What would they miss? Indeed, would virtually the entire community say, "What will we do now?" How many people will say in the shock of learning of the church closing, "Where will we turn? They were the ones who always . . . "?

It is in answering such a question that we may discover clues about the current state of our church. We may come to see some of the reasons for our strength or weakness as a faithful community of faithful disciples. The question can function as a kind of annual missional integrity audit.

A Church That Decided Not to Grow

A church once decided not to grow. Some churches do that without a great deal of effort, but this church worked very deliberately not to grow. They had run out of building space. They had run out of parking space. They had run out of land. There was no more land to buy. At the time relocation did not appear viable. Their space did not adequately serve their current membership. So they decided, "We will stop growing."

Because of that decision, even though they did not have a good location within their community, there were no directional signs anywhere on the streets or highways. They had no brochures. They did no advertising. They had no prospective member visitation. They had no new member classes. The pad for attendance registration did not include a column "wish to join the church." When people said, "We would like to join your church," they received brochures about the other churches of their denomination in the area. The only people received into membership were the people who insisted and almost demanded to be members. Even the sign in front of the church had incorrect times for the worship services, though this happened by oversight, not plan!

With all these efforts to discourage growth, the church continued to grow. The reason was the involvement of this church and its members for over twenty years in every imaginable aspect of mission in that community. Whether it was with people who were homeless or hungry or sick or destitute, anywhere you turned in that community, you found the people of this church. Because of that commitment, when people moved into the community, the powerful word of mouth about this church drew them. The congregation would not give up these mission involvements. So they frantically tried to understand, "Why is it we cannot stop growing when we are working so hard at not growing?" There is a lesson here. If you want to thrive— serve. That is leadership in the Wesleyan spirit.

A Tough Time to Be a Christian

This is a difficult time to be a Christian. The world is insisting on an accountability not required when the church was so dominant culturally. People expect behavior to match belief, performance to coincide with preaching, and impact to follow intent.

Why is it we have such a powerful example from Jesus and the Wesleyan tradition and yet often continue such parochial lifestyles in our churches? Why is it that we find ourselves more concerned with the church's institutional needs than with the needs of people both inside the church and outside?

Could it be that we are operating with the mistaken notion that God's primary interest is religion? God is not primarily interested in religion. God's primary interest is everything.[7] God is the creator and sustainer of all life and all creation. There is no distinction between sacred and secular, if by that one means that there are some spheres outside the love, care, and sovereignty of God. However, once we assume that God's primary interest is religion and religious activities, then instead of becoming an instrument of servanthood, the church sets itself up as an object of loyalty. Thus we set ourselves up to be God rather than to serve God.

One of the literal meanings of the Greek word translated as deacon or servant is "a waiter of tables." We tend to think of ourselves and the church more as the restaurant owners than the waiters. "We are happy you are here; we hope you will come again," we say. The biblical image is to wait on the tables of the dying and hurting of the world. This service expects nothing in return except the joy and fulfillment of emptying our lives for others in the name of Christ. That is the Wesleyan vision of servant ministry.

A district superintendent called me late one Saturday asking me to preach the following afternoon at a small church on a circuit in the district; the pastor had had a sudden illness. The church was on a narrow gravel road many miles from the nearest main highway. There was no parking at the church. The building was very small and needed repair. There was no piano. There was no running water. The pulpit chair was an inexpensive plastic-covered easy chair. Even the church sign, such as it was, had the name of the church misspelled.

Despite all this, the people started coming. They kept coming until the church filled. Parking was all along the road, in yards, and in fields. Even though there was no musical instrument, the singing was marvelous. During the service, as they shared joys and concerns, I came to understand the magnetism of this church. This was truly a community where when one suffers, all suffer, and when one rejoices, all rejoice. People were genuinely pulling together to meet the needs of one another. When that is the case, the church is always strong and vital, even when the financial and physical resources are minimal to nonexistent. Why? Why was there such life in this church? It is for the same reason Wesley reached people. The spiritual and human needs of people were paramount. There is a connection between what is happening in church and the needs of people.

DOING WHAT JESUS DID

Shortly after seminary I was pastor of a church where Bishop J. Waskom Pickett came to speak as a part of a district mission emphasis. He told how, as a young man in his early twenties, he went to India as a missionary with high hopes of converting vast numbers of people. The people welcomed him warmly. They came to hear him preach. However, the people did not respond to his invitations to become Christians. During his first year he baptized only one person. He feared this woman simply felt sorry for him. The answer he felt was to work harder on his sermons. He spent hours trying to improve his preaching. Still none responded.

Then one evening during his devotional time, he came across a very simple statement that said we are to do what Jesus did. He took a sheet of paper and drew a line down the middle. On one side of the line he wrote what Jesus did. His entries included preaching, teaching, healing the sick, giving sight to the blind, helping the lame to walk. Then on the other side of the line he began to list what he was doing. There was only one entry: preaching.

That night he wrote the mission headquarters asking that

a doctor or nurse be sent to work with him as a team. After the new coworker arrived, the preaching on Sundays continued. Now, however, during the week they were healing the sick, restoring sight to the blind, and helping the lame to walk. It was at that point that many people became Christians.

Why the change? Had they discovered some trick or gimmick? No. They had simply rediscovered what is clear in the gospel and in the Wesleyan tradition. As Albert Outler described it, "The world hears the gospel when it sees it—when its witnesses are clearly concerned with human existence and clearly committed to a more fully human future, in this world and the next." They had rediscovered what it means to be servants of God.

A LEGACY OF SERVING

The Wesleyan movement began not for itself but for others. Thriving and serving were indeed linked. The growth of the Wesleyan enterprise is directly related to its identification with the needs of all God's children.

Is this happening today? Are people saying that because our church is in the community, there are no hungry people? Are people saying that because of our church's presence in the community, there is no bigotry or discrimination? Are they saying that because we are in the community, there is no one homeless?

Such questions continue to be the test for heirs of the Wesleyan spirit.

CHAPTER FOUR
Remembers Especially the Poor

> " . . . *the choicest part of London society: I*
> *mean the poor.*"
>
> —*John Wesley's letter to Brian Bury Collins, June 14, 1780[1]*

LEADERSHIP FOR THE POOR

A story told by Jim Wallis, founder of the Sojourners Community in Washington, D.C., illustrates the centrality of the poor for God's people. The story took place during Wallis's seminary years. He tells of a study he and several friends undertook. They sought to find every reference to the poor and oppressed in the Bible. At the end of their study they identified over 1,200 verses addressing God's concern for the poor in the Old and New Testaments. One of Wallis's friends took a beat-up, old Bible and spent several weeks with scissors removing all of those verses.

Wallis concludes the story by holding up the Bible, full of holes, with all references to God's care for the poor removed. He says, "Our Bibles are full of holes. The poor have been cut out of the Word of God. This is an issue of integrity for the church. . . . It is the poor who will reveal Christ to us."[2]

How do we know what is an appropriate Christian vision for leadership? How do we know what God is calling us to do? We learn through the same sources from which we come to know all of God's will for us. Scripture is primary. We also draw from experience, tradition, reason, prayer, worship, meditation, and other Christians. Most of all, we come to know God's purpose for us through that standard beside which everything else stands—Jesus Christ.

JESUS' EXAMPLE

Consider the model of Jesus' own ministry. Think about the setting in which he went to minister. The context for Jesus' ministry resembled a circle that included some people and excluded many others. The people on the inside felt that God drew the circle, choosing them to be on the inside and others on the outside. The people inside the circle were "good people." They knew and kept the law, attended worship, and tithed.

Many others remained outside the circle. Poor people were outside the circle. The sick were outside the circle. People of different religious, racial, and ethnic backgrounds were outside. Sinners and tax collectors were on the outside. Women, to a great extent, were on the outside of the circle.

So Jesus came into this social context and announced: "These are some of my priorities. First of all, I have come 'to preach good news.' " At that moment many people sighed with relief. "Thank goodness we finally have a *spiritual* leader," they must have said. However, as we know, Jesus continued. "I have come 'to bring good news to the poor . . . to proclaim release to the captives and recovery of sight to the blind, to let the oppressed go free, to proclaim the year of the Lord's favor' " (Luke 4:18-19).

Many were upset by these words. Despite such provocative words, the listeners remained calm. They had seen preachers come and go. They knew that bold words do not necessarily mean that anything happens.

Jesus was different. His leadership matched his proclamation. Word started getting around about conversations with women of the street. He had lunch with a tax collector. He made a Samaritan the hero of one of his stories. He cared for the sick.

What are we seeing here? What clues from the ministry of Jesus do we discover for our leadership? It is as if Jesus is saying, "God has sent me to proclaim God's love to all people. I choose to go first to those most in need, to those outside the circle."

Is this favoritism? No. It is not favoritism in the sense that God loves some people more than others. Strategic concern is a more apt description. There is a shepherd with one hundred sheep (Luke 15:3-7). One is lost. What does this good shepherd do? The good shepherd goes and finds the lost sheep. But think of the ninety-nine. They could say, "Wait, this is favoritism. This is a kind of affirmative action for lost sheep. What about us? We did not get lost!"

How does the good shepherd respond to such questions? The good shepherd reminds us that the one sheep is not loved more than the ninety-nine. Rather, the one lost sheep is the one in need. This is not favoritism. It is strategic concern.

WESLEYAN EXAMPLE

On the Sunday before Christmas several years ago, a television evangelist was rehearsing the political events of the past year. Things had not gone well for him and others who shared his political values, he maintained. The forces of evil had won too many victories. Those fighting for the right, as he was, were under siege. He completed the message with a financial appeal in light of these circumstances. "Make a Christmas gift to Jesus," he encouraged, "and send it to me at the address on the screen."

I had read just the week before some words of Wesley

with a different suggestion. To early Methodists Wesley implored this use of money: ". . . first supplying thy own reasonable wants, together with those of thy family; then restoring the remainder to me, through the poor, whom I had appointed to receive it."[3]

John Wesley heard the gospel message of good news for the poor. He felt a mandate to reach the poor, often the unchurched in his day. From Oxford days, Wesley made a practice of visiting the poor as a spiritual discipline. He encouraged—indeed, insisted—that other Methodists do the same. The poor remained at the heart of how Wesley understood his leadership throughout his life. Even in old age Wesley risked his own health and well-being to seek funds for the unemployed and others in need.

As a "theologian of experience" Wesley believed in "the immersion in lived experience." Theodore Jennings elaborates on how important it was for Wesley that Christians spend time and energy with the poor. Such direct interaction is essential to understanding and identifying with them. Thus, the regular practice of "visiting" the poor, sick, and imprisoned was essential.[4]

Jennings believes this "constant practice of visitation" saved Wesley's concern for the poor from becoming merely sentimental or ideological.[5] There is something about experiencing the reality of suffering firsthand that exposes how out of touch sentimentality or ideology is to the actual needs of people. There are limitations to Wesley's approach, but there is no doubt that, for him, it was the poor themselves who remained paramount. They maintained priority over the feelings or ideas of those seeking to help.

Wesley's move to field preaching came not from an intellectual commitment so much as from an emerging practical necessity. Despite real reservations, Wesley yielded to encouragement to try field preaching for the sake of the gospel and those excluded by conventional worship.

Nothing about field preaching fit who John Wesley was, except his calling as a bearer of God's good news for the poor. He adapted his more natural personal leanings for the sake of the message.

Wesley was not comfortable, at least at the beginning, with this new medium. But he caught on quickly. On his first major occasion of field preaching on April 2, 1739, Wesley's understanding of his hearers was clear. He chose for his text: "The Spirit of the Lord is upon me, because he hath anointed me to preach the gospel to the poor" (Luke 4:18 KJV).[6] Wesley thereafter used field preaching as a powerful means to share the love of Christ.

Wesley practiced a profound "gospel egalitarianism."[7] Outler cannot name "another Englishman of his century . . . who so heartily identified himself with the English poor or whose identification was more heartily accepted by them."[8] In his journal Wesley once recorded the following thoughts: " 'Tis well a few of the rich and noble are called. O that God would increase their number! . . . If I might choose, I should still . . . 'preach the gospel to the poor.' "[9]

Some evangelicals, according to Bishop Kenneth L. Carder, "found their constituencies largely among the rising middle class and lesser nobility." Wesley, on the other hand, "planted the Methodist societies in pockets of poverty and nourished them with the gospel of justifying and sanctifying grace."[10]

PILGRIMAGE TO RESPECTABILITY

According to Nathan Hatch, "identification with the people" represented the "genius of evangelicals" in eighteenth-century America. However, Hatch documents how by the 1840s Methodists in America (by now the largest Protestant denomination) had undertaken their own "pilgrimage to respectability." It was perhaps "Asbury's signal achievement" that he had for so long preserved the missional quality of Methodism from the "inevitable allure of respectability."[11]

For many, the legacy of Wesley and Asbury lingered on, but their church was changing. The rough and tattered early days of American Methodism gave way to "more refined and educated versions of Methodism." Even as these changes brought prosperity and greater ease, there were many who could never forget nor betray "the movement's original birthright of being a haven for ordinary people."[12]

Hatch describes the change in populist religious movements by the mid-nineteenth century as a "metamorphosis from alienation to influence." In 1852 eleven of Indiana's thirteen congressmen were Methodists; the governor and a senator were as well. Churches were building large sanctuaries, installing organs, and demanding better trained clergy.[13] Earlier in the century, upon the selection of Methodist preachers as chaplains to a state legislature and Congress, Asbury warned: "So; we begin to partake of the honor that cometh from man: now is our time of danger. O Lord, keep us pure, keep us correct, keep us holy!"[14]

Nathan Bangs, an influential preacher in the first half of the nineteenth century, was one who saw Methodism becoming popular establishment. "Middle-class propriety and urbane congeniality" now tempered faithfulness to the movement's original passion and zeal. "If Asbury's career represented Methodism's triumph as a populist movement, with control at the cultural periphery," says Hatch, "then Bangs's career illustrates the centripetal tug of respectable culture." Hatch observes how dissenting movements have often, in America, "doubled back toward learning, decorum, professionalism, and social standing."[15]

The changing character of Methodism obviously had benefits. There were also problems. A gap began to develop between Methodism and some of its constituents. Some church divisions took place. Other denominations and movements began as a result of these struggles.

Class Tensions

Numerous factors contributed to the divisions. Issues often cited are theology, social issues, and polity. However, in reviewing that history, one gets a sense that class and economics played a far greater role, even if not always a public one, in what happened to the church. Indeed, one Wesleyan scholar has gone so far as to say that practically *none* of the denominational fragmentation reflects primarily doctrinal issues, except for the "holiness" controversy. Most splits, Outler contends, ran "along lines defined by ethos, social, ethnic, and structural issues."[16] Even the divisions between northern and southern churches that occurred within Methodism and other denominations in the mid-nineteenth century as the nation divided over slavery involved much more. "In the long run," says Hatch, "fault lines of class, education, and social status within a single denomination may have been more significant than sectional tension, even between northern and southern churches."[17]

While this view may make too little of both theological and social issues, it does describe well the class dimension of these divisions. As Methodism pursued its "pilgrimage to respectability," it became increasingly difficult for some to feel at home with Methodists, even as some Methodists felt increasingly uncomfortable with them.

The experience of African Americans that led to separate denominations for many gave an early signal that class and race would supplant, to a great extent, the early egalitarian Methodist model. Bishop Daniel A. Payne of the African Methodist Episcopal Church captured what was to become a familiar story for African Americans and the poor:

As long as this Church were in number few, and in condition poor, its colored members were gladly received and kindly treated, but as soon as it began to increase in numbers and wealth, so it became elevated in social position—with this increasing prosperity, the enslaved and proscribed free Negro became contemptible in its eyes.[18]

While more respectable Methodists were "dressing up" to go to church, the Free Methodists were deliberately "dressing down" for church, lest the poorer members become uncomfortable. It is true that abolition, prohibition, and pew rentals were some of the issues involved in the Free Methodist movement. However, the prominent Free Methodist leader B. T. Roberts made it clear that recapturing the Wesleyan passion for the poor was behind this church:

> The claims of the neglected poor, the class to which Christ and the Apostles belonged, the class for whose special benefit the Gospel was designed . . . will be advocated with all the candor and ability we can command.[19]

To understand the Church of the Nazarene one must appreciate its roots in the "holiness movement" in the United States. However, the focus of this church was clearly on the poor who were being neglected, in their judgment, by Methodism. Clergy such as Phineas Bresee left "successful" churches within Methodism to minister more freely among the poor. The very name Church of the Nazarene sought to communicate an identification with the poor. This church was to be a place for rich and poor alike.[20]

Most of the divisions did not make a major statistical difference for the larger Methodist denomination. This fact may have given mainline Methodist leaders reason to disregard these movements and what was happening to the Wesleyan witness. They might have observed, however, that these movements represented, as Finke and Stark put it, "a valid portent of troubles to come."[21]

SEPARATION OF THE ELITES

The gap that began to develop between Methodism and the poor in the nineteenth century became a massive gulf in the twentieth century. The same is the case for other mainline denominations. These denominations so associated with the development of the country now mirror the larger American contemporary problem which John Gardner has called the increasing "separation of elites."[22]

The privileged in the church, education, government, and elsewhere have lost touch with less privileged people. The established institutions, many of which—like Methodism—made their mark through service, now appear to increasing numbers as unconnected and "not with us."

Leaders of almost all Wesleyan bodies today would admit what a struggle it is to remain focused on the poor. Most have to contend with their own versions of a "pilgrimage to respectability." So it is with humility that all of us come to seek renewed inspiration and direction from the strong, though ambiguous, Wesleyan legacy.

Bishop Kenneth L. Carder illustrates the dilemma and possibilities for a new identification. In the church he served before election to the episcopacy there is "a small group who gather on Thursday evenings for worship. Most of the thirty to forty who attend live in the streets and local shelters. . . . One cold winter evening a man came to the service barefoot. Immediately we all noticed. The more affluent among us began to scurry around to find shoes for him. We couldn't find any in the church. The stores were closed, so we couldn't go out and purchase them."

Then a man who lived in nearby low-income housing "went to the shoeless man and said, 'Take my shoes. I have another pair at home.'" This group member "did spontaneously," Bishop Carder said, "what those of us who had several pairs of shoes never thought of doing."[23]

THE CHALLENGE TODAY

What does this heritage mean for Wesleyan leaders today?

The statistics about the poor in America continue to be staggering. Over thirty million Americans live in poverty. Even more devastating is that children are the poorest Americans. Forty percent of the poor are under the age of eighteen. Almost 50% of the "chronically poor" are children.

In the last decade the second-fastest growing category of housing in the United States was mobile homes. (The number one category was prisons!) Mobile homes have tended to be "emblematic of life on the margins of American society—geographically, economically and culturally." The growth rate was 60%. Today one in seven residences in the United States is a mobile home. One out of every sixteen Americans is living in one.[24]

If there is a gulf separating United Methodism and most of the poor, then the numbers on each side of the gulf are not even. There are many more poor. Is this not a clue for a church struggling to find its way?

Donald Dayton maintains that Wesley never developed a systematic theological articulation for his passion for the poor. He sees the absence of such a theological grounding as a major flaw in Wesley's theological legacy and one reason for the later ambiguity found in the Wesleyan movement.[25] This may be true, though Wesley is not entirely silent about his theological rationale. It is also true that we see here, as in other cases, a better Wesleyan example in the lived reality than in the formal articulation.

We in the church need to hear again the call to serve the poor. We are called not to be served, but to serve. Colin Morris, the former president of the United Church of Zambia, tells about the day a Zambian man died not two hundred feet from his front door. The pathologist said that the man had died from starvation. His shrunken stomach contained only a leaf and what appeared to be a clump of grass.

Later that day Morris received his church newspaper in the day's mail. Its pages contained the white heat of indignation. What was the cause of the indignation? Was it the fact that some people are starving while others enjoy overindulgence? Was it the fact that many children begin the race of life many laps behind simply because of circumstances of their birth? No. The indignation resulted from yet another publication delay for the last report of the Anglican Methodist Study Commission.

All this was too much for Colin Morris. The paradox was too great. Here was the church preoccupied with its institutional in-house concerns and interests, while people died at the very doorsteps of the churches. He said of this incident, "Little men with shrunken bellies call the church's bluff."

THE "INVISIBLE" PEOPLE

One of the tragedies of religious demagoguery was the 1978 deaths of over 900 followers of Jim Jones in Jonestown, Guyana. Under pressure because of abuses within the People's Temple compound, Jones led his followers in a mass suicide/murder ritual. There was one particularly frightening statistic related to that disaster. Two years after the deaths, there were still 251 bodies not claimed. When I read of that I asked myself, "Who are the people in my community who, if they died today, would have no one to claim their bodies in the next two years? Are they in my church? Do I know who they are?"

It was intriguing to hear some of the descriptions of Jones's movement by people who started out with the movement but left toward the end and thus survived. When they first went to his church, many thought that they had "died and gone to heaven." It was a place where people who had been nobodies were somebodies. They were loved. They felt acceptance and care.

These are the people who are not in our churches. One needs simply to compare some statistics about communities and churches to find the "invisible" people in our communities who are not in or touched by our churches. Compare the rates of adult illiteracy in your community and in your church. Compare the percentage of children present. Compare the percentages of persons with disabilities. Compare the percentage of single persons. Compare the racial and ethnic makeup of the community with the church's.

A pastor went to a new appointment. On the first Sunday morning the congregation was waiting for the pastor to come from the study to begin the service. When the pastor did not appear, an usher went to the study and saw the pastor standing next to the window.

"Pastor," the usher said, "we are ready to begin." As the pastor turned, the usher noticed tears running down the pastor's cheeks. "What is wrong?" asked the usher. "Are you ill?" The minister replied, "No. I was just looking out in the alley at all of those dirty little children playing." The usher, with dropped head, replied, "Oh yes, I know what you mean, but you will become used to it." The pastor replied, "I know I will. That is why I am crying."

There are things to which all of us have grown accustomed. There are things we see every day, but we never truly see. There are things we know, but we never actually know. We need to help one another open our eyes, open our ears, and open our hearts so that we might be leaders faithful to the Wesleyan spirit.

COMING TOGETHER FOR THE POOR

The literature of the Salvation Army includes a picture of William Booth waving to his wife, Catherine, inside a

Methodist church. Booth is motioning for her to follow him in a symbolic departure reflecting impatience with the failure of the church to meet the needs of the poor.[26] Such an image hurts. It is a reminder of both the glory and the failure of the Wesleyan commitment to the poor. If our history makes for humility, it also reflects a powerful force on behalf of the poor that will not die. New Wesleyan leaders in every generation reclaim the solid Wesleyan social location among the poor and downtrodden. That is our calling today.

Here is another case where our Wesleyan theological and historical heritage can help. If evangelism, social issues, and theological stances have become ideological battlegrounds, then it is the poor that should bring us together. This does not denigrate the legitimacy of the debates. It does put them in perspective—biblical, historical, and Wesleyan.

For example, two pastors in the Wesleyan tradition might have taken different theological paths along the way. Different theological streams nurtured them. They went to different theological schools. They read different theologians. They subscribe to different journals. They go to different caucus meetings. Indeed, these two pastors represent archetypes of polarities in Wesleyan theological and social thought. Neither has had an ambiguous theological thought since leaving seminary!

However, if these two pastors are serving in the same community, they will encounter each other regularly. They may not see each other at the bookstore or clergy study group. On the other hand, these two pastors, if they are true to the Wesleyan tradition, will bump into each other regularly among the poorest of the poor of that community. *That* is leadership in the Wesleyan spirit.

—PART TWO—

PRACTICES OF LEADERSHIP IN THE WESLEYAN SPIRIT

CHAPTER FIVE
Practices Multiple Leadership

MULTIPLE LEADERSHIP

In the New Testament, many persons assume leadership roles and offices. Such leadership positions, though, never become exclusive possessions of individuals. They never become private property. Rather, the leadership responsibility remains always with the total community of faith. At various times different people may fulfill these responsibilities because of changing circumstances. At no time does the leadership position become anything other than a trust from the larger community.

Leadership exists on behalf of and for the sake of community. In the Bible, titles and offices carry with them authority from the community. There are also community understandings of responsibilities that accompany such offices. The community of faith expects faithful stewardship of these responsibilities. Honor and authority are never separated from responsibility and effectiveness.

The experience of Isaiah in the temple (Isaiah 6) is often portrayed in very individual terms. Surely there is a powerful sense of personal conviction, confession, and forgiveness in this spiritual event. Isaiah confronts the very holiness of God. Isaiah hears the voice of God calling him to service. This was a personal call to leadership, but the leadership to which Isaiah responded was far from individualistic. The call came out of community and was on behalf of community. The very familiar question to Isaiah was, "Whom shall I send, and who will go *for us?*" (Isaiah 6:8, emphasis added).

Think of multiple leadership as a dynamic and fluid understanding of leadership. Leadership emerges from different people at different times in different ways. The phrase "multiple leadership" comes from Mary Parker Follett. Max DePree uses the concept "roving leadership" for a similar approach. Letty Russell speaks of a "temporary inequality" that takes place within organizations. What appears as inequality is actually a moment in which certain persons lead, followed by other times in which others lead.[1] Such is not a rigid or arbitrary allocation of leadership tasks. It is a creative way of working together as needed and appropriate to accomplish a shared vision.

WESLEYAN EXAMPLES

From the beginning of the Wesleyan movement, many people functioned as leaders. People from different social locations helped lead this passionate movement of God. There was no one route to leadership in the Wesleyan ranks. Leadership came from Church of England priests and also from a stonemason, a printer and publisher, a baker, a cobbler, and a schoolmaster.[2] Leaders were male and female, ordained and lay, of noble birth and modest origin, black and white.

In the Wesleyan tradition, the example of multiple leadership is not perfect and not always consistent. Yet there are some very clear pointings in this direction.

LAY PREACHERS

One example is the use of lay preachers. If the question were asked in Wesley's day, "Where does one look for religious leadership?" the answer would surely have been,

"Among the ordained." The concept of leadership for lay preachers was not an ordinary and customary way to approach leadership in the church. Yet among Methodists, a form of multiple leadership emerged through the lay preachers.

Experience, more than reason or temperament, drew John Wesley to multiple leadership. As with so many issues in his life, Wesley was genuinely torn between competing claims. To his credit, most of the time he came down on the side of what was best for the most effective proclamation of the gospel. Wesley's own words seemingly argue both sides of many debates, including those regarding leadership. The distinctive character of the Wesleyan movement, though, bears witness to the spirit that prevailed.

The story of Thomas Maxfield, as recounted by Richard Heitzenrater, illustrates Wesley's struggle. Maxfield had a religious experience under John Wesley's preaching in Bristol. He then began traveling with Charles Wesley to the societies. At some point Maxfield began to preach to the society in the absence of the Wesleys. Henry Moore later reported the story of what happened next.

"Thomas Maxfield has turned Preacher," Wesley complained to his mother. While Susanna Wesley did not generally approve of lay preaching, her response reflected her ambivalence. To her son she cautioned, "Take care what you do with respect to that young man, for he is as surely called of God to preach, as you are. Examine what have been the fruits of his preaching, and hear him also yourself." Wesley, it is reported, "bowed before the force of truth."[3]

Methodism could not have grown in numbers and expanded geographically apart from lay preachers. It was two lay preachers, Richard Boardman and Joseph Pilmore, whom Wesley sent to America in 1769. It was lay preachers who first introduced the Wesleyan message of God's prevenient, justifying, and sanctifying grace to vast areas of the United States. Peter Cartwright never let anyone forget this.

He appreciated that Wesley "providentially saw that to accomplish the glorious work for which God had raised him up, he must . . . send out his 'lay preachers' to wake up a slumbering world." Cartwright feared that if Bishop Asbury had waited for a "choice literary band of preachers, infidelity would have swept these United States from one end to the other."[4]

The leadership of lay preachers was a natural extension of the egalitarian spirit and pragmatic approach of the Wesleyan movement. An ideology of leadership did not motivate the change. It was shaped by a passion for the gospel of Jesus Christ. John Wesley appreciated the Anglican tradition and his Anglican roots. Even more valuable to him was the need to spread the message of Christianity to effect personal and social holiness among persons and nations.[5]

Not only did lay preaching exist, it indeed became "the hallmark of American Methodism."[6] Lay preachers led much of the growth of early Methodism and have continued to be a characteristic of the Wesleyan tradition through the years.

WOMEN

It would have been equally "obvious" for many in Wesley's day that religious leadership was male leadership. Yet the leadership of women in the church, both in England and America, provides another example of a more expansive understanding of who exercises leadership.

Many leaders of the early societies and classes were women. It was quite common for women to outnumber men among society leaders. Women were also preachers in England and America. Jean Miller Schmidt has studied the history of women in American Methodism. "One of the surprises of my research," she reports, "is discovering that the preaching and spiritual leadership of women occurred much earlier than I, or other scholars, had previously suspected. . . . Women were experiencing a call to preach the gospel and some of them were becoming traveling preachers (not, of course, ordained) as early as the 1810's and 1820's."[7]

The faithful witness of Methodist women did not represent anything new in Christian history. Rather, as Paul Chilcote observes, women leaders of early Methodism were more "a unique manifestation of a recurring theme" from the day of Resurrection and beyond. He also notes that the "prominence of women is conspicuous in every era of revival in the history of the church."[8]

Chilcote identifies some of the factors that "contributed to Wesley's early appreciation of women's gifts" for church leadership. Primary influences were "his mother, the legacy of the Puritan heritage, his rediscovery of the practices of the early church, and his friendship with the Moravians." Moreover, the spirit of the movement "was one of both spiritual and social liberation. The Wesleyan revival . . . was a barrier-breaking movement."[9]

The leadership of women as ordained preachers never did become ordinary practice in Wesley's time. But an expanded leadership role for women did become a way that multiple leadership emerged in unexpected places. The practice was not perfect or consistent. There is, however, a clear pointing toward multiple leadership. This direction developed more fully, though not without struggle, in the years to come.

CLASS

Conventional wisdom in Wesley's day limited religious leadership even further. There were class limitations in the thinking of church leaders that narrowed the scope of potential leaders.

The multiple leadership of the Wesleyan movement began to break down some of the barriers of class. Indeed, much of the success of the Wesleyan revival came precisely because of its ability to reach beyond what we might call today the "traditional constituencies" of the church. Methodist leaders emerged from almost every walk of life and circumstance. The movement not only survived the opening of leadership to people who were different from and less experienced than traditional leaders; it actually thrived and flourished precisely because of such leadership. An extensive cadre of different, committed, and disciplined Methodist leaders presented with energy and effectiveness God's invitation to discipleship to all kinds of people.

Ernst Troeltsch has reminded us, "To the middle and lower classes [Methodism] brought a new sense of the sacredness of personality."[10] Outler believed this sacredness of personality emerged in leadership responsibilities assumed in the class meetings. Many people participated in leadership. Much of the success of the Wesleyan movement came from the small groups. All members assumed a high level of leadership responsibility for each other and the group. Many of the participants, as Outler has pointed out, were seen as faceless and worthless in the streets outside. But in these groups, a whole generation of future leaders for the church and society found respect, dignity, and status. Through this new sense of worth, together with experience from previously unfamiliar leadership roles, they discovered a new vision of God and of their own potential as leaders for God.[11]

Annie Dillard captures the power of human potential discovered:

> I had been my whole life a bell,
> and never knew it
> until at that moment
> I was lifted and struck.[12]

RACE

In America as in England, those on the margins of society heard the Wesleyan message with joy. From the beginning of the American Methodist movement, African Americans were among those who sought hope through the Wesleyan message. African Americans were a part of classes and societies, and their numbers grew.[13]

African Americans served as lay preachers, although functioning under restrictions different from those of their white counterparts. They received licenses as local preachers and later as traveling preachers. The presence of African American preachers was unusual among most denominations. African Americans knew this fact well. When local laws forbade African American preachers, the category of "exhorter" became the designation for many African Americans who functioned as preachers.

Contemporary Methodists may never fully appreciate the contributions of early African American preachers. It took "remarkable courage, tact and finesse," according to William B. McClain, for a black man to be a preacher at such a time.[14] In addition to the struggles encountered by all Methodist preachers of the time, they also faced the dangers of a dehumanizing social situation that often appeared to be getting worse instead of better.

One of the most popular of these preachers was Harry Hoosier, known as "Black Harry." Thomas Coke once described Hoosier, who could not read, as "one of the best preachers in the world." John Stewart is a notable figure in missions because of his pioneering work among Native Americans. Henry Evans was a skilled church organizer. Richard Allen and Jarena Lee were outstanding preachers in the African Methodist Episcopal tradition. From the well known to those now lost to history, African American leaders have contributed significantly to the Wesleyan movement.[15]

Such leadership is an example of multiple leadership in that it emerged from a source not considered for leadership in many other churches. As with all our examples, the presence of leadership across racial lines was incomplete from the beginning. Just as other nontraditional leaders faced only limited opportunities for leadership within Methodism, African Americans faced these and even greater obstacles because of race. Yet, despite the failures, the faithful example of African American leadership in the midst of difficult circumstances continues to call us to view leadership in our time in more open ways.

A DIRECTION BUT NOT A MODEL

"Those who stood on the fringe of English society often found their way to the center of the Wesleyan Revival," according to Paul Chilcote. "Methodism created its own leadership from within. It empowered the masses of working class and common people, and women, and trained them to be effective servants of the Word."[16]

"Wesley's parish was not only without boundaries and his congregation without pedigree," says Richard Heitzenrater, "but his concept of ministry was without limits so long as the activities fit into his vision of scriptural Christianity by helping a person receive the wholeness that God's salvation could bring to humanity."[17]

There is much to affirm in the Wesleyan tradition that reveals at least glimpses of multiple leadership. Wesley's focus on linking leadership and calling, and his insistence that the fruits of ministry be considered in determining the integrity of one's leadership, led him to a more democratic spirit than some others. However, it is also true that Wesley's approach to expanding leadership was generally an accommodation to the "extraordinary calling" of people. The "normal" structures stayed unchanged for the most part.

One must acknowledge the many violations of the principle of complete and inclusive multiple leadership both in England and America. The indignities endured by African Americans provide some of the clearest examples. The divided Wesleyan witness today is the result of, and bears witness to, sins of the past. Laity, women, and lay preachers have all had to struggle for full acceptance as leaders. In many ways the struggle to make the spirit of multiple leadership a reality continues today and will into the future. Yet, we still find in the Wesleyan movement, and in Wesley himself, more of the spirit of multiple leadership than one might commonly expect for the time.

ALL ARE LEADERS

Multiple leadership helps to address the myth that some are leaders and others are followers. The reality is that all are leaders, and all are followers. The genius is to know when to be which. In the course of any day, all of us are constantly going back and forth between being one and being the other.

Mary Parker Follett tells of a new elementary school teacher at a particular school. There are agreed-upon policies and procedures at this school regarding what teachers do at the end of the school day pertaining to the chalk, erasers, and chalkboard. Despite clear and repeated instructions, the new teacher did not follow them.

Many days went by. Despite numerous reviews of the correct procedures, the instructions did not result in action. Finally the custodian came in one afternoon and, once again, began explaining the policies and procedures about the chalk, erasers, and chalkboard to the teacher. The teacher, seemingly oblivious to the explanation, continued to pack to leave. The custodian, noticing the apparent lack of interest, stopped midway through the instructions. He said to the teacher, "Excuse me. Apparently you are not accustomed to working under the supervision of a custodian."

The custodian was right; the teacher was wrong. The teacher thought, "I am leader." The teacher was right in the sense that the teacher is leader much of the time. In this particular situation, however, the teacher was the follower and the custodian was the leader. It was the custodian who had worked with everyone to develop those policies. It was the custodian to whom everyone in the institution looked to fulfill this calling of leadership.

Letty Russell reminds us that "there are never too many leaders, for power is not understood as a zero sum game."[18] Rather, power and leadership gifts multiply when shared. Think of power not as a fixed sum like a pie; that is, the larger the piece of pie you get, the smaller the piece I must get. Instead, think of power as an "expandable pie." In another of God's strange calculations, the larger the piece of power you have, the larger the pie becomes and the larger the piece of power I have.

In other words, the more I am willing to be influenced by you, the more willing you will be to be influenced by me. Thus, giving power and receiving power are part of the same experience of practicing multiple leadership. From this perspective there can never be too many leaders. Indeed, power and leadership gifts multiply when shared and many persons become leaders.

There is a potential downside for this shared leadership and authority. When there is no compelling and unifying vision throughout the church, there tends to be a dispersal of energy in many different directions, offering little power or impact. If multiple leadership is to be the rule, then it is essential to make sure that God's vision for the church at this time in history is discerned, articulated, and shared.

MULTIPLE CENTERS OF LEADERSHIP

All of us are leaders. All of us are ministers. All have a ministry. Ministry belongs to the whole people of God.

This truth came home to me dramatically through an

incident that I learned about when I was in England a few years ago. In London there is a Roman Catholic priest named John who had a dream of having a ministry with some of the lowest paid workers in London. When after several years his assignments never made this possible, he took a job as a street sweeper. Without anyone knowing that he was a priest, he found his ministry each day among coworkers. This worked out wonderfully.

He was a bit older and a bit slower than the other street sweepers, and at the end of every day there was work that he had not completed. The other street sweepers would come together and help finish his assigned work. They did not mind because they discovered very quickly that even though John was a bit older and a bit slower than the rest, he was a very good talker. When they had trouble with wages or working conditions, they would explain it to John and he would talk for them to the powers that be.

One morning John came to work and a small group of coworkers was waiting as they had done on many other occasions with some problem. Today their faces held more anguish than usual. They said, "John, something terrible has happened. Joe was found dead this morning." Joe was a forty-year-old coworker. He had died in a homemade shed in an alleyway. They said, "If we had only known. If we had only known that Joe had nowhere to live, we could have helped him. If we had only known Joe was sick, we could have done something. If we had only known Joe was having hard times, we could have helped in some way. Now it is too late. Joe is dead. We will never be able to do anything for Joe."

John said, "Maybe you are wrong. Maybe it's not too late to do something for Joe." They said, "What do you mean? He's dead. How can we help Joe?" John said, "At least we can give him a decent funeral." They responded, "That is a wonderful idea, but we would not know where to begin to

———✦✦✦———

have a funeral." It was at that moment when John revealed that he was a priest and that he would help them plan a funeral.

At the end of the week, Joe's funeral took place in a church arranged by Father John. Street sweepers from all over London came for that service. John, now dressed as a priest, presided at the service. When the service was over, but before anyone got up, one of the street sweepers sitting near the front stood and looked out over this sea of street sweepers. With a dazed and puzzled look on his face he said, "How many more priests are there here?"

That is the question of Christian discipleship. That is the question of Christian leadership in the church. The question is not, "Whom will we select for high positions?" That is an important question, but it is not *the* question. The question God is asking us in the church this day is, "How many priests, how many ministers, how many leaders for God are there throughout the church?"

It is significant how often there is multiple leadership during periods of church renewal and vitality—whether for a local church or for a denomination. It is in such times of revisioning and revival that whole generations of different leaders emerge for the church and society. It is in these eras that conventional assumptions about who can lead do not stop this multiple leadership from flowering, unlimited by class, gender, race, and ordained status distinctions.

So it was in the Wesleyan renewal tradition that a whole generation of leadership—multiple leadership—emerged from which church and society benefited for decades and generations.

James Kouzes and Barry Posner capture this spirit well in introducing their new edition of *The Leadership Challenge:* "Liberate the leader in everyone, and extraordinary things happen."[19]

CHAPTER SIX
Leads from the Center and the Edge

In many ways John Wesley represented the center of establishment. He was a "university man" as were other key leaders of the early Wesleyan movement. Nevertheless, by choice and calling he moved to the edge. We know of the productive and lifelong ministry Wesley had with those on the edge of his society. Troeltsch observes that Methodism "gained its victories in the middle and lower classes."[1]

Wesley would preach to university students and then preach to miners. He felt free to modify liturgical practices and hymnody to reach "all sorts of people."[2]

While leading from the edge effectively, he stayed connected to and appreciative of the center. The choice was not exclusively center or margin for Wesley. It was precisely because of Wesley's grounding in a theological and liturgical center that he had the freedom to change. He could distinguish between what is essential in the faith and mere "sensibilities" related more to one's culture and class than to the gospel.[3]

AMERICAN EXAMPLE

In American Methodism there are some of the clearest examples of leading from the center and leading from the edge, but they have tended to occur more sequentially than simultaneously. The church tends to lead in a way that is shaped by its place within the society. When relegated to the margins, leading from the edge is the only option. When placed at the cultural center, leading from that strength is logical, but such leading often loses the dynamic tension of the Wesleyan witness.

LEADING FROM THE EDGE—THE "MOST INSIGNIFICANT" RELIGIOUS BODY

An example of leadership from the edge comes from the late eighteenth century. In 1776 only 2.5% of church members in America were Methodists. Over 55% of church members were Congregationalist, Presbyterian, and Episcopalian. Some even predicted on the basis of current trends that within 100 years virtually all church members would belong to these three denominations.

There was virtually no college-educated clergy leadership among Methodists. Members of the establishment were attacking Methodists. The president and faculty of Harvard earlier had issued a unanimous "Testimony against the Reverend Mr. George Whitefield," a Methodist evangelist. The noted preacher Lyman Beecher harbored similar opinions. Such feelings came out at a gathering held in connection with the Yale commencement in 1814. Beecher said, with Methodists very much in mind, "Illiterate men have never been the chosen instruments of God to build up his cause."[4]

Nathan Hatch reminds us of the marginal position of these church leaders. He refers to them as "outsiders, interlopers and marginal men." Yet they "created the turmoil, defined the issues, formed the organizations, and preached the gospel that captured the hearts and minds of so many citizens in the following century."[5]

So it was that when Francis Asbury said in 1797, as he did on many occasions, that Methodists "must draw resources from [the] centre to [the] circumference," he had more than geography in mind. Asbury wanted Methodism to be a faith of the people. Hatch notes that he "worked tirelessly to embrace the lowly, white and black, and to transfer resources from the center to the periphery of the movement." Asbury insisted that clergy leadership required that one lay aside all the "trappings of a gentleman"—including dress, manners, and material security. "We must suffer *with* if we labor *for* the poor," he said.[6]

The historian William Warren Sweet captured the marginal status of Methodism of this era. "Of all the religious bodies in America at the close of the American Revolution," he said, "the Methodists were the most insignificant, in point both in numbers and of influence." They were, according to Sweet, the "smallest and most humble religious body" in America.[7]

FROM EDGE TO CENTER

Wesley, Asbury, and others feared and warned against the kind of "pilgrimage to respectability" that was to take place in much of the American Wesleyan movement. Wesley once asked, "Does it not seem (and yet this cannot be) that Christianity, true Scriptural Christianity, has a tendency, in process of time, to undermine and destroy itself?" His rationale was, "For wherever true Christianity spreads, it must cause diligence and frugality, which, in the natural course of things, must beget riches! And riches naturally beget pride, love of this world and every temper that is destructive of Christianity."[8]

One of the most colorful and successful of the pioneer Methodist preachers in the first half of the nineteenth century was Peter Cartwright. On one occasion Cartwright was speaking of those denominations that insisted upon an educated clergy:

> [They] used to contend for an educated ministry, for pews, for instrumental music, for a congregational or stated salaried ministry. The Methodists universally opposed these ideas; and the illiterate Methodist preachers actually set the world on fire, (the American world at least,) while [the others] were lighting their matches![9]

By the middle of the nineteenth century, even as Methodists became the largest Protestant denomination in the country, the value of church property among Methodists was still relatively modest. All that was to change. William Warren Sweet traced the increasing wealth and respectability of Methodists through the nineteenth century. During the second half of the century, some of the most noticeable indicators of this affluence were the rise of clergy salaries, increased spending on the construction of churches, and the growing prevalence of pipe organs.[10]

LEADING FROM THE CENTER—"THE MOST IMPORTANT OF ALL"

Clearly the nineteenth century provides examples of leading from the center. In 1866 *Harper's Weekly* claimed that Methodism had become "the predominant ecclesiastical fact of the nation."[11] It is amazing to find examples of leadership from the center so close in time to the marginal life. We need only go to the mid-nineteenth century and incidents that involved President Abraham Lincoln and Methodist Bishop Matthew Simpson.

At the time of the 1864 General Conference, church leaders decided to send a message to President Lincoln. A delegation set out to deliver that message. One member of the delegation, Dr. Moody, thought that it would be good for the President to have a copy of the message prior to their meeting. In this way the President could respond when the delegation arrived.

Moody went ahead of the delegation, and the day before their arrival he went to see the President. He told Mr. Lincoln's private secretary that he must see the President immediately. He informed the aide that on the following day a delegation of ministers representing "the largest, most loyal and influential church in the country" would call upon the President and present a message. Moody immediately saw the President.

The next day when the delegation arrived and presented their message, President Lincoln presented them with a letter of reply. His message to them said, "While all churches are important, . . . it may fairly be said that the Methodist Episcopal Church . . . is, by its greater numbers, the most important of all."[12]

Upon the assassination of President Lincoln, Mrs. Lincoln called for Methodist Bishop Matthew Simpson. Bishop Simpson was becoming something of a symbol of the emerging respectability and influence of Methodism in America. He represented in many ways the new place of Methodism at the center of American culture. During the administration of five presidents, he was among the first citizens of the country.[13]

Bishop Simpson had prayer at the White House before the removal of President Lincoln's body. He then traveled with the body to the burial. At Springfield, Illinois, he made a major address. He served in the role of public preacher very well. In Springfield he said of the slain President: "Chieftain, farewell! The nation mourns thee. Mothers shall teach thy name to their lisping children. The youth of our land shall emulate thy virtues. Statesmen shall study thy record, and from it learn lessons of wisdom. . . . Hero, martyr, friend, farewell."[14]

The following year Bishop Simpson recalled the progress of Methodism in America. Speaking at a church in New York City, he said:

> Call to your mind a little gathering a hundred years ago of six poor, obscure persons, in the lower part of the present city, meeting to sing and pray, little thinking that so great a Church would spring out of their efforts. Contrast its present condition. Look at our commodious churches, our large congregations, the wealth, the influence, the refinement, the great enterprise, and we see that a mighty work has been accomplished, and we can well exclaim, "What hath God wrought!"[15]

This is the same church described a few years before as "the most insignificant" of all the churches.

FROM CENTER TO EDGE

The twentieth century has seen radical changes in the American religious landscape. The sociologist Robert Wuthnow calls it the "restructuring of American religion." Historian Martin Marty talks of "seismic shifts" shaking the churches. Theologian Harvey Cox speaks of a "deregulation of religion" in recent times.[16]

The "mainline" denominations of today followed different paths to that designation. Some were close to the American establishment from the beginning. Others, including The United Methodist Church, began on the margins of society, only later to become a part of the nation's religious and cultural center. However it was that each arrived, they functioned as an informal "established" church. This is no longer the case.

The changed place of the mainline churches today is obvious. There has been movement from the center of establishment toward the margins. Many assume this movement is bad. It is clearly different, but not necessarily negative.

This new social location puts churches closer to the early church and early Methodist situations, since being at the center of the establishment was hardly the early church experience. Warren Carter discusses the marginality of early Christians described in Matthew. He acknowledges that mainline churches are experiencing more and more of this reality of marginality. He also sees hope in this. This new-found marginality may offer "possibilities for what it means to be disciples of Jesus in these times and places."[17]

The movement from center to edge is more a direction than a completed reality. It is more the description of a movement taking place. William R. Hutchison speaks of this era as a "between the times" moment. "Between the times" refers to a "gradual and somewhat painful adjustment from one social reality to another" by the mainline churches.[18]

Walter Brueggemann uses "exile" as a metaphor for the current situation. Exile is not primarily geographical but social, moral, and cultural. Mainline Christians increasingly experience a sense of "homelessness" in this place "between" establishment and total disestablishment. Carefully avoiding withdrawal and sectarian tendencies, Brueggemann contends that "baptized exiles" will in these times lead lives of "endless negotiation" with both center and edge. He reminds us of biblical characters who were remarkably "bilingual." They knew the speech of the empire and were willing to use it, without ever forgetting the cadences of their "mother tongue" of faith.[19]

The cultural center for which mainline churches served as the unofficial established church no longer exists. It will not return. "Mainline Protestantism must stop trying to be the established church for the cultural center," claim Kirk Hadaway and David Roozen. "American society is a pluralistic conglomeration of individuals and competing subcultural groups, loosely bound by pragmatic realities and secularized morality."[20] However, to ignore the continuing influence and power of mainline traditions, particularly by some churches in certain regions, is also to misread the current situation.

EDGE AND CENTER TOGETHER

Richard Bondi contrasts leading from the center and leading from the edge. He advocates leading from the edge, but not without careful regard for the center. Similarly, Rosita deAnn Mathews speaks of "power from the periphery" for African American women and their leadership. At the same time she is careful to point out that these leaders should also "utilize power from the center to make change."[21] Such images may help in a moment in which the mainline churches experience elements of both the center and the edge at the same time.

Bondi maintains that the edge and the center pair in "a difficult bond. There is movement and vitality on the edge, but power and stability at the center. Leaders who live only at the edge can become detached from their communities and unable to lead." Those leaders who "commandeer the center can end up protecting its interests from the dangerous opportunities of the edge." For Bondi, however, the more dangerous temptation is to try to live always at the center: "Stability without movement leads to stagnation and eventual collapse."[22]

Effective leadership, then, is not so simple as choosing center or edge. Bondi captures the inevitable tension. "For the truth is," he says, "that if we cannot bring ourselves to tell the story truthfully in the center, we will never be able to tell it from the edge."[23]

Carter speaks of this tension in the New Testament. Being a part of, yet apart from, was crucial to the New Testament view, he concludes. The New Testament's stance is not so much a sectarian stance from which the church runs mission forays. Such a stance would privilege separateness.

Rather, the concept of living *both* at the center *and* the edge is closer to the reality of New Testament people. They lived in the cities. Their writings utilized conventional images. They sometimes met in the homes of wealthy patrons or members since the buildings where most of them lived were too small. Yet they were also different and on the margin.[24]

Whatever else the mainline churches in America are today, they are not sectarian. They are no more sectarian than they are establishment. Therefore, a view of leadership that takes seriously leading from the center and the edge—together—makes sense.

LEADING FROM THE CENTER AND THE EDGE

A student in one of our leadership classes, Eduardo Bousson, developed a helpful diagram showing how margin and center can be very deceptive concepts if seen in isolation from one another. What is marginal may be the center at the same time.

For example, in the midst of the civil rights revolution in the United States, Martin Luther King Jr. represented for many a prophetic voice from the margins. From the margins with the poor and dispossessed, he called America to live up to the nation's ideals. At the same time King came to represent within the civil rights movement the more established centrist approach, with others pushing from the margins of that movement. Reminiscent of strange descriptions of Wesley, King was called a "conservative militant" by August Meier during the civil rights struggle, to acknowledge the crucial leadership role King played amidst competing factions.[25]

Every margin may, in another context, be a center, and every center, a margin. So it is for many church leaders today. Almost simultaneously they must lead from both margin and center. The dilemma of the church has always been to lead from both the edge and the center at the same time. Wesley's example is one of trying to hold both together and in tension. That continues to be the challenge.

Struggle, tension, and ambiguity characterize Wesley's relationship to center and edge. Donald Dayton identifies in Wesley's legacy a "profound ambiguity of countervailing forces." He notes that, on the one hand, there was Wesley focusing on the poor in field preaching and in establishing churches among the poor, working classes, and lower middle classes. On the other hand, there is the Methodism of respectability that had the effect of pulling itself away from the poor as it moved closer to the center of culture. This ambivalence has been present almost from the beginning. It certainly has marked many successive generations. At times, as Dayton notes, one emphasis will carry the day. At other times, another emphasis will prevail. The history of the Wesleyan movement, says Dayton, "must be interpreted in terms of this struggle in the very soul of our movements."[26]

Today's church leaders do not have the luxury of choosing either center or edge as the sole location for leadership. The context to which God has called us is not so neat. There are times when faithful leaders will lead from the center as good stewards of the strength which that stance affords. At other times the same leaders will lead from the edge, identifying with the emerging call of God found in the edge's weakness and vulnerability.

One temptation is to stand on the edge or in the center for the wrong reasons. One may be on the margins by default or neglect. What Gregory Jones says about the place of theology is also true of church leadership. "The margins . . . need not be a bad or unchristian place to be; but theology may be marginalized partly for the wrong reasons, because we are failing to fulfill our vocation and responsibilities."[27] Likewise, one may stand in the center out of cultural accommodation. One striking example of this recurring pattern in church history comes in Christine Leigh Heyrman's study of Southern evangelicals in the eighteenth and nineteenth centuries. She describes a minority religious movement that "colonized a culture—and was colonized by it in turn."[28]

Both the center and the edge offer opportunities to serve God so long as one never forgets the limitations and temptations of each. When leaders remain grounded in God and the power and justice of Christ, their leadership can and should be challenging, even in such a "between the times" moment of history.

CHAPTER SEVEN
Lives in a Tension

Leaders in the Wesleyan spirit seek to hold together and in tension a host of seemingly competing and incompatible commitments. These include personal holiness and social holiness, doctrinal responsibility and doctrinal freedom, law and gospel, worship and service, piety and action.

This approach led Wesley to argue different sides of the same issue on different occasions. Such seeming inconsistency created great tension for Wesley. His emphasis depended on what was missing in the debate at that time. He considered which way he needed to lean in that situation. So when people heard one part of what Wesley said— and did not understand the larger context—often there was misunderstanding. There were so many positions in which he saw truth and value. There were also many things about which he had questions. He was willing to be a leader who lived in that tension.

INEVITABLE TENSION IN WESLEYAN LEADERSHIP

It is easy to see how Wesley's approach led to confusion and misunderstanding. Many had trouble understanding how he could argue different sides of the same issue. "In a given controversy," Heitzenrater observes, "Wesley at times found himself having to defend or emphasize one side of such a tandem set, often at the apparent expense of the other." Tensions sometimes resulted.[1]

Such tension is not always comfortable for a leader. It means such a leader is at times the voice of tradition and at other times the voice of the "not yet." In some situations the leader is the most conserving force and in other situations the most liberating. At times such a leader is the defender of a position and at other times the critic. Bishop Matthew Simpson, an extraordinarily influential Methodist leader of the nineteenth century, was such a leader by some accounts. He "bore the penalty that every careful and discriminating thinker and leader must pay," according to one writer, "of being misunderstood and ill appreciated on both sides."[2]

Ralph Ellison captures this dilemma in a powerful way near the end of his classic novel *Invisible Man*. This story of the denial of the humanity of African Americans closes with the narrator saying: "So it is that now I denounce and defend. . . . I condemn and affirm, say no and say yes, say yes and say no."[3]

If one side of the balance is lost, or one side overemphasized, then the wholeness, richness, and genius of the basic Wesleyan synthesis disappears. Needed today are not so much ideological leaders as leaders who take with equal seriousness their own values and the context of their leadership.

Leaders function in the midst of competing values. The competition is not so simple as the leader's values against the values of others. Indeed, leaders embody within themselves, or should, many value commitments that create tension. Careful and prayerful discernment day by day and situation by situation is essential.

To ask the question "Which way should I lean in this situation?" is not a surrender of integrity. Integrity does not mean doing and saying the same thing in every situation.

There must be consistency of overall values and goals; indeed, a key test for leaders always is whether they wear the vision they articulate as naturally as they wear clothes. However, different occasions call for different responses. The test in any situation is not a legalistic consistency. It is the pressing needs in this particular moment.

Giving attention to which way one should lean as a leader in a given circumstance is not "playing to the gallery." The question one is asking is not "What do people want?" It is not "What do people expect?" Rather the question is "What is most needed?"

Theological educator Kevin LaGree speaks of leadership in the church as an art form. "To be an artist it is important to know much and know it well," he says. "It is also important to know how what we know is changed by where we are." That is one of the most important lessons for leaders. It is crucial to have knowledge, but it is as essential to be attentive to how that wisdom is in dynamic interaction with changing contexts. Wesley demonstrated this lesson well.

Wesley, for example, worked as hard as anyone ever did to know what true doctrine was. Yet when Wesley stood to preach, he did not begin with the true doctrine that he had worked out so carefully. He began with the particular congregation to which he was speaking. Beginning with their needs, he then drew from the richness of his doctrinal work just the word most needed for them in their situation. This meant that in the same day Wesley would find himself preaching many different messages. The change was not because his position was changing but because the needs of groups of people were different. His understanding of what was true, just, and right was not changing throughout the day. But the needs of the people called for different leadership. The context was different so he needed to "lean" a particular way.

Holding in tension may mean advocating or questioning

in ways unfamiliar to us, but ways that the situation requires in order to preserve the wholeness of the truth. When we abandon the tension, we are no longer leaders toward a greater truth. We are merely partisan advocates for a part of the truth. This is one reason the church and our society have not been served well by either the Old Left or New Right. Each takes partial truth with no tension and presents it as the whole truth.

Robert Bellah uses Abraham Lincoln and slavery to illustrate such tension in leadership. Some radical abolitionists were willing to abandon the union in order to eliminate slavery. They often argued for secession of the free states from the slave states. This would have salved the conscience of the North. It would also have left the slaves more firmly fixed in their chains than ever. This option was appealing to many. But Lincoln knew that the goal was not to feel good. The goal was to abolish slavery and save the union. It was Lincoln's "moderate yet uncompromising stand," according to Bellah, that weathered the criticism of virtually all sides to achieve both values.[4]

The Wesleyan Search for "Third Alternatives"

Tension was never an end in itself for Wesley. It resulted in large part from Wesley's preference for "third alternative" solutions. This is a concept that I first learned from Albert Outler. He felt that Wesley utilized a way of "third alternative theologizing" that amounted to "*a special method* all its own." For Outler, understanding this method was "crucial for any really fruitful interpretation of Wesley as theologian."[5] Wesley's theology provides third alternatives to "all the barren polarities generated by centuries of polemics."[6]

Third alternative refers to Wesley's refusal to see competing claims as the only options. Neither was mere compromise a solution. Compromises are often weak and finally unacceptable to everyone. Compromise usually postpones the real issue. Rather the task is to create a new option. This third alternative seeks to preserve, not weaken, the key strengths. At the same time it endeavors to avoid the weaknesses of the competing positions.

Heitzenrater reminds us that Wesley "embodied ideals and qualities not always easily held together or reconciled."[7] A sampling of these includes knowledge and vital piety, revival and social welfare, evangelicalism and sacramentalism, justification and sanctification, faith and works. Perhaps this is why scholars often portray Wesley with such peculiar descriptions. "Radical conservative," "romantic realist," "quiet revolutionary," and "reasonable enthusiast" are some examples.[8]

Indeed, Mary Elizabeth Moore speaks of Wesley's "theology of contrasts" as a major contribution. Wesley's refusal to address only one side of an issue and his willingness to hold together radically different positions is "exceedingly promising" for people today who face a world as full of contrasts as his.[9]

In Wesley one finds "the genuine integration of what seemed to some of his critics as nothing better than a 'medley of . . . Calvinism, Arminianism, Montanism, Quakerism, Quietism, all thrown together.' "[10] Yet there was a "certain genius in Wesley's ability to forge a dialectical synthesis." He always resisted "a one-dimensional message of grace."[11]

Mary Elizabeth Moore writes about United Methodist theologian Georgia Harkness and her theological legacy in similar terms. "As a searching, integrative thinker, Harkness carried on the Wesleyan tradition of seeking to understand and respect diverse points of view. She attempted to hold these views together when possible, and she sought to reform one point of view through the influence of others, or to find a middle ground where diverse views could be integrated."[12]

Perhaps this is the reason Harkness spoke of herself theologically as an "evangelical liberal." These terms represented for her as much an approach to theological reflection as a doctrinal stance. She believed that it was possible to combine "tolerance with decisiveness, open-mindedness with Christian conviction." For her, "such an attitude leads both to knowledge and to power."[13]

Mary Parker Follett, though not a theologian or a Wesleyan, wrote in a similar vein in 1924. She used the concept of integration. "The truth does not lie between the two sides," she said. "We must be ever on our guard against sham reconciliation. Each must persist until a way is found by which neither is absorbed, but by which both can contribute to the solution. Integration might be considered a qualitative adjustment. Compromise, a quantitative one."[14]

Follett understood, as Wesley did, that one should resist the temptation to mistake compromise for the true integration of a third alternative. The greatest deficiency of compromise is that there is no real change in one's own thinking. Integration, on the other hand, guards against what Mill called the "deep slumber of a decided opinion."[15] As my teaching colleague at Saint Paul School of Theology Susan Sonnenday Vogel reminds students, "There is nothing so dangerous as an answer—if it is the only one you have!" One of the great advantages of integration is the personal change that takes place. We come to understand and appreciate the ideas and values of others. Partisanship, says Follett, "starves our nature." We are so intent on our own values that other values are starved out of us.[16]

In the same spirit Letty Russell speaks of "God's new math." This new math of partnership includes "looking for the third thing." In contrast to "my thing," third-thing thought looks for the commonality on which to build. Russell advocates this new divine math that includes the "gift of synergy." In such math there is not primarily addition taking place. Rather there is a multiplying effect that causes the whole to become much greater than the "sum" of the parts.[17]

Many examples emerge from Wesley himself and from early Methodism. In Wesley's time some advocated a kind of doctrinal dogmatism. Others reflected what amounted to doctrinal indifferentism. The great strength of dogmatism was responsibility. The great strength of indifferentism was freedom. Instead of working a compromise, Wesley sought to preserve the strengths of both responsibility and freedom.

He did so by holding the options together and in tension. Carefully avoiding the weaknesses of the extremes, he advocated a third alternative in which one was free to believe but not free from belief. In this stance one must know what one believes, articulate those beliefs, and give reasons for them. One also must be willing to share that with others once a week, and listen to other people. Freedom of Christian conscience is maintained. One is not free, however, from the doctrinal journey. One is not free for doctrinal irresponsibility.

Take another example. Wesley saw one theological option as Calvinism. The Calvinist approach put its emphasis on God and God's actions. Recovering a strong doctrine of the sovereignty of God mattered greatly to the Calvinists. Wesley saw the Catholic theological stance as another option. The Catholic approach in Wesley's day put its emphasis primarily on human responsibility and activity. The role that people play in the act of salvation received considerable attention.

What Wesley did was to draw from both positions. God initiates the faith journey. God reaches out through prevenient grace before we ever know of God's love. But human beings also have a role. That role is not to earn, create, or deserve salvation. It is to accept the gift of salvation. But accept that gift we must. So Wesley holds the evangelical and Catholic strengths together. God's sovereign grace and human agency in salvation combine in this third alternative.

Wesley took ideas, concepts, and values available to everyone. He then put them together in a unique way. His task was not discovering new truths. It was looking at existing truths with a more open and integrative perspective. Outler described him as "a clear-headed synthesizer of a rich, multifaceted tradition—that very rare sort of eclectic who actually understood the options he had to choose between."[18]

As leaders in the Wesleyan spirit who are seeking third alternatives, as opposed to compromise, we must find ways to keep people from facing off against each other. Our calling is to find ways in which people with different ideas will instead turn together, as if toward a blank chalkboard. It is in such a stance that a third alternative is most likely to emerge. In this posture it is more likely that parties will draw from the strengths of alternatives while avoiding their weaknesses.

THE TYRANNY OF THE OR

The complexity of most realities makes it essential to seek something like Wesley's third alternatives. All of us face competing claims and values. They may not be equally important, but some are crucial. Some values and claims appear to be direct competitors with each other. Do we relocate or do we stay and become more invested in the community? Do we use limited resources for a new staff person in music or youth? Do we feature music that the music director wants or that desired by the congregation? Should small-membership churches have priority because there are so many of them or should this attention go to large-membership churches where most of the people attend?

The temptation for a leader is to select from among the various competing options. Some do so based on personal values. Others may respond to political pressure from others. In either case, the result may be disastrous for all involved. Most people will choose sides if issues become framed as competing options requiring choice. If leaders join them on one side or another, there is little hope for a congregation to minister faithfully and effectively. Leaders should seek to raise questions that can help lead to genuine third alternatives wherever possible.

James Collins and Jerry Porras speak of the oppression caused for leaders by the "tyranny of the OR," and the liberation leaders experience with the "genius of the AND." This genius is "the ability to embrace both extremes of a number of dimensions at the same time."[19] This sounds very similar to Wesley's third alternative approach.

Like Wesley, they are not talking here about balance or blending. They are seeking to preserve competing values.

LEADING FROM THE CENTER WHILE AVOIDING THE MIDDLE

We often think of the middle as a place of safety, comfort, and weakness. So it often is. Yet the edge can also be safe, comfortable, and weak when everything is too certain and we talk only to people who agree with us.

An alternative image may be leading from the center while avoiding the middle. Such a stance escapes the middle of compromise, common denominators, and avoidance of hard issues.

There is a center that is not the middle. It is the center where there is power. There is power because there is focus. For church leaders, that center is Jesus Christ. From the clarity of this center we are freed for genuine inclusiveness and diversity. A focused center makes it possible to draw God's wisdom from many different sources. We can draw from many sources without fear because the center is in place and not threatened or debated. It is in this kind of center that we find corporate strength. Here gifts are drawn from many different places but centered always in Jesus Christ.

It is indeed helpful to discover that the clearer we become about where we stand, the freer we become. We can now permit others to stand at different places, if God is so leading them at this moment in their lives. We are able to stand together and learn from one another.

Yes, the middle can be an escape but so can the edge. Barbara Brown Taylor, a noted Episcopal preacher, tells of a local Ku Klux Klan member. On the front seat of his car is last Sunday's church bulletin alongside a Bible with an embossed leather cover. She goes on to say that Klansmen are not the only people who try to capture the word for their own narrow purposes. There are lassos flying all over the place, she says, each of us trying to harness a little horsepower for our own cause. Some insist that the word of God is a literal word or a liberal word or a masculine word or a feminine word. Some claim it is a word only for the poor or only for the rich or only for those who speak our own language.[20]

One task of a leader is to do just what Taylor is doing here: to name the lie that God's wisdom is synonymous with my wisdom. Danger awaits when God's truth becomes synonymous with my group's wisdom, my particular theology, my particular politics, or my particular place in life.

What then about legitimate and deeply held differences? They remain. But something has changed. The issue is no longer one of melting down every position to get to a common denominator. Rather there is the freedom for one position to stand in its strength alongside differing positions.

When Paul says in Galatians that there is neither Jew nor Greek, slave nor free, male nor female, that is not a statement that these differences no longer exist. Those differences are still present. There are still issues to address. The key point is that we are now one in Christ Jesus. No longer are these differences the primary ways that we define ourselves. Rather we define ourselves in terms of what we have in common—the Christ who is at the center. Once we no longer define ourselves strictly by our differences, we are in a better position to acknowledge and deal with the differences that are there. There is now a greater opportunity and willingness to address the differences instead of ignoring them.

Where there is no central focus, there is a vacuum. As Margaret Wheatley and others have helped us see, space will be filled. If not filled with a focus that can bring us together, the space fills with our differences, which simply become larger. So the only definition we can have, the only basis for conversation, will be the difference.

When there is that central unity, differences remain but are put in perspective. They do not define our basis for being. Instead of being a liability, our differences define a richness from which to draw because a part of God's wisdom is represented in all. God's wisdom is never found totally in any one place among God's people.

Leaders in the Wesleyan spirit neither fear nor glamorize tension. They understand that tension is the natural arena for leadership. The task of leaders is not to resolve the tension through victory for one side or through compromise. Leaders see the tension interspersed throughout with the presence and wisdom of God, just waiting for God's new creation to emerge. Often a third alternative becomes the "new thing" God is doing in our midst.

CHAPTER EIGHT
Seeks to Include

Aristotle understood that similar people cannot bring great cities into existence. Wesley understood that a vital religious community required the richness of different kinds of people and different understandings of God's wisdom. Wesley's approach to ideas and people became a way to include rather than exclude. Among those he sought to serve, the diversity of ideas and people was genuine.

The goal of inclusion is unity of purpose, direction, and commitment, but never uniformity. Without a unifying center, inclusion becomes only a gathering of unrelated differences. Inclusion in the Wesleyan spirit requires a common foundation.

Unity is more like-mindedness than likeness. In fact, there is danger in gathering only with those who are "like me." Like-mindedness is never a given. Rather, we "grow our own like-mindedness," Follett reminds us.[1] It can never be assumed. Neither can it be maintained without constant vigilance. Clarity about the basis on which we as diverse people with diverse ideas come together must always be at the forefront of our thinking.

DIVERSITY OF IDEAS

As we have seen, Wesley sought to hold different, and often competing, claims together with integrity. He did so because he felt a kinship with many different people and perspectives. He saw much to value in traditions not his own. Consequently, he desired to preserve and incorporate those values. His commitment to third alternatives (described in the previous chapter) helped to provide a vehicle for inclusion.

While Wesley could be passionate in opposing positions different from his own, his basic instinct was to identify in other positions that from which he could learn. Mary Parker Follett put it this way, "Our opponents are our co-creators, for they have something to give which we have not. The basis of all cooperative activity is integrated diversity."[2]

Georgia Harkness reflected this Wesleyan spirit. She sought always to be open to more truth from "whatever source it comes." She felt it was possible "to live by the truth one has and to let others differ" as they believe. To do so, one must hold together and in tension "tolerance with decisiveness, open-mindedness with Christian conviction." For her this was the path that "leads both to knowledge and to power."[3]

Wesley's "theology of contrasts," as Mary Elizabeth Moore calls it, is as useful today as in Wesley's time. His refusal to address merely one end of contrasts is needed today as never before. Contemporary debates often engage persons who are passionately committed to different poles of an argument but are missing the Wesleyan tension. "Such theological discourse," says Moore, "represents a tendency to harden and argue doctrines rather than to live in the dynamic of contrast. Such theological reflection contributes more to death than to life."[4]

Thus, Wesley's approach bridged many divisions within Christian thought and practice. Wesley's concern was to find alternatives to what Outler once called the "barren polarities generated by centuries of polemics."[5]

Too often churches and church institutions have not

sought to bridge such gaps. Indeed, well-meaning Christians have sometimes been the source of greater division and distrust. Distrust among Christians seems to generate more fear than the forces of evil with which we all contend. More hurt than redemption and reconciliation occurs in such an atmosphere. As a result, the base on which such churches and institutions stand has become smaller and smaller. While desiring to include others, we have, through some of our practices, made others feel unwelcome around the table.

Two seminary students from different theological stances within the Wesleyan family were talking one day. One said to the other, in a rather condescending way, "You need to change your theology so you can be about justice." The second student reframed the discussion. He suggested that the question for each of them is the same, "How does your theological stance inform and make possible the calling of Christ to be about justice?"

A study of churches experiencing social and community change found that, with few exceptions, theological categories are not good predictors of how a church will deal with such change. "Being liberal or conservative was not the key to whether and how people adapted to ethnic, economic and other changes," according to researcher Nancy Ammerman. "More important than where the congregation *started* theologically was its willingness to use the resources of its theological tradition to help it interpret the situation. Adapting congregations actively worked at using their symbols and stories in new ways."[6]

The Wesleyan movement did not begin as a doctrinal debate. Doctrine always served the task of introducing people to the love of God and making possible a saving encounter with Jesus Christ. It served growth in the love and knowledge of God and social witness. Doctrinal interpretation—together with evangelical proclamation, discipleship formation, and social witness—became an inseparable component of a vital relationship to God.[7]

DIVERSITY OF PEOPLE

Wesley was always reaching out to those who were different. Diversity was a challenge for him and early Methodists. Yet the results make clear the seriousness with which he took the task. Wesley sought out those who were different socially and economically. He especially sought a church open to sinners who felt rejected by society and God. "Outcasts" of all, "to you I call," he says in a hymn. God's arms are spread "t'embrace you all."[8] It is this word of grace, hope, and invitation that the world so needs to hear from the church today. In a world of polarization and self-interest, a church seeking "to embrace you all" is indeed good news.

Early American Methodists could have focused exclusively on the majority population. Instead, they chose to be multicultural in a land that did not yet know the word or the reality. Hatch points out, "More African Americans became Christians in ten years of Methodist preaching than in a century of Anglican."[9]

Here, as in many other historical examples, the record is a mixed one. Such examples do not represent models to replicate. Rather they help provide a spirit to continue to "grow into," even when that growth requires acknowledging and repenting for limitations. "We must continually bathe all that is past," Dietrich Bonhoeffer wrote from his prison cell, "in a solution of gratitude and penitence."[10] For example, the Christmas Conference in 1784 did call for the abolition of slavery in America. However, within one year, accommodation to slavery began. The historical circumstances around the formation of other churches, especially

African American Wesleyan denominations, but also others, represent clear examples of racism and classism existing alongside more inclusive directions. Still the Wesleyan spirit at its best can continue to inform our leadership today.

THE REALITY OF DIVERSITY

The need for a renewed spirit of inclusion of people is crucial today. Roozen and Hadaway contend that, next to the aging of the baby boomers, "the increasing racial/ethnic diversity of the United States will be the major demographic trend through at least the first quarter of the new century."[11]

Joel Kotkin and Yoriko Kishimoto describe the United States of the future as a "Post-European America." The country will indeed be a "world nation" with "ties to virtually every race and region on the planet. By the end of the United States' Third Century, an absolute majority of Americans may be descended from people who came from somewhere other than Europe."[12]

There are several reasons for the fast-growing racial diversity of the United States. Differing birth rates and immigration patterns are key factors. The last census showed growth rates for the decade. African Americans grew by 13%. The Hispanic population grew 53%. The number of Asians and Pacific Islanders more than doubled. The Native American populations grew 38%. The "other races" category grew by 45%. During the same years, the white population grew by 6%.

By the middle of the twenty-first century, according to the U.S. Census Bureau, 53% of the population will be non-Hispanic whites, down from 74% today. At the beginning of the twentieth century non-Hispanic whites constituted 90% of the population.

In contrast, Hispanics will make up 24.5% of the population, up from the current 10.2%. Asians will make up 8.2%, up from 3.3% now. African Americans will constitute 13.6% by midcentury, up from the current 12%. These are predictions that may change, but the direction of diversity is unmistakable.[13]

America is experiencing "one of the most dramatic shifts" in racial and ethnic makeup, says Steven Holmes, since the slave trade transformed the racial composition of the South and immigration gave an ethnic flavor to many urban areas. Even the Baby Boom years following World War II never reached the growth levels that are expected for Hispanic and Asian population increase over the next thirty years.[14]

In any one year, approximately 800,000 legal immigrants and 300,000 illegal immigrants come to the United States. More immigrants came in the last fifteen years than in the previous fifty years. Between 1970 and 1994, immigrants rose from 4.8% of the population to 8.7%. Most important for diversity is that the new immigrants come from different countries than the old. In the 1950s, two-thirds of a much smaller number came from Europe and Canada. By the 1980s, nearly half came from Mexico, other parts of Latin America, and the Caribbean. Almost 40% came from Asia.[15] Barely 10% of newcomers are from Europe.[16]

The racial/ethnic proportional population growth is particularly striking among the young. Sam Roberts projects that by perhaps as early as the end of this decade, "blacks, Latinos, and Asians may constitute nearly a majority of the nation's children."[17]

By 2020, according to projections by demographer William Frey, in twelve states—mostly in the Plains, upper New England, and the intermountain West—more than 80% of those under seventeen will be white. By this time there will be another twelve states—including California, Texas, and most Northeastern states, in which whites under seven-

teen will be a distinct minority.[18] The Census Bureau fore-
casts that in thirty years non-Hispanic whites will make up
less than half of the people under the age of eighteen, but
three-fourths of those over sixty-five.[19] The youthfulness of
this growing diversity makes its impact much more significant for the future. The implications will not be apparent to
church leaders if they are not giving attention to these
changes.

C. Kirk Hadaway puts the challenge for the mainline
churches pointedly. He maintains that "one key for future
growth . . . of mainline denominations" is "to reach beyond
their traditional white constituency—without losing it."[20]
And reach beyond we must. Clearly the church's vitality in
the next century will be shaped to a great extent by its willingness and ability to respond to the changing face of
America.

Jesus Christ as the Unifying Center

Diversity is not something to endure but, rather, to cele-
brate. Diversity is always a challenge but one offering many
rewards. "All diversity wisely handled," Follett maintains,
may lead to the "something new" that all creative leaders
seek.[21]

However, in a community of faith, more has to be said.
Just as we know that people can be homogeneous and
unfaithful, so also can people be diverse and unfaithful.
Diverse people of faith must hold something in common
that is stronger than all their differences. That may be why
Emilie Townes says that the starting point for work on
diversity in the church must always be prayer and fasting.[22]

In her inaugural address at McCormick Theological
Seminary, President Cynthia Campbell, acknowledging the
seminary's diversity, said, "We must admit that diversity in

and of itself is not enough to hold a community together. Bringing together people who have not traditionally been together before . . . is a good thing to do. . . . But staying together, working together, growing together mean that a diverse community must find a center, a common ground, a core of commitment."

Letty Russell maintains that every partnership, whether of a few or thousands, requires a center. The center is the basis of commitment and gives strength and identity to the members. Commitment to the center is what allows persons to be open to others without feeling threatened. Without this central commitment as the source of unity and strength, people return to what Russell calls the "old math." Old math features adding and subtracting but misses the multiplication of possibilities and opportunities that can only come from creative interplay and synergy.[23]

Frederick Buechner speaks of his seminary days in the 1950s at Union Theological Seminary. While not diverse by today's standards, his experience, Buechner says, was one of utter diversity of theology, politics, countries, cultures, and visions of the church. "But beneath all those ways in which we differed from one another there seemed to me to be something deep and life-giving that all of us shared." He found this reflected in Latin words over the door of the dining hall: "They knew him in the breaking of the bread."[24]

INCLUSIVENESS AS A CONSEQUENCE

Indeed, all true inclusion comes as a consequence of a shared common center. Diversity and inclusiveness flower best not so much as ends in themselves but rather as by-products of a faith that unites all kinds of people more tightly than any differences can separate. This may be one reason why some churches that lift the virtues of diversity regularly exhibit so little of it, while other congregations talk little about diversity yet display a richness of racial, economic, and cultural differences in their lives. "Churches that unite people across cultural barriers," says Carl Dudley, "can name the deeper religious source of their unity, the source that makes their diversity possible."[25]

Leadership in the Wesleyan spirit finds unity in Christ, despite countless differences. Such unity in Christ maintains distinctiveness and self-identity, but the differences are put in the new perspective of the common center of Jesus Christ. Such leadership maintains unity through respect for others as valued children of God. As in other cases, the example of the Wesleyan tradition is to hold together concepts and people not normally associated with each other.

So many more might experience the community of faith if we could hold together knowledge and humility, because the more we learn, the more we realize how limited our knowledge is. So much would happen if we held together passion and perspective, because the clearer we become about our own values and beliefs, the freer we are to permit space for the other's point of view.

As leaders in the Wesleyan spirit, may we all grow in both knowledge and humility. May we become more passionate about the truth of what we believe and also gain a broader perspective in which to place our beliefs. May our own convictions become stronger and deeper, even as we grow each day in our respect for others for whom God has not revealed wisdom in the same way.

CHAPTER NINE
Makes "Connection" Happen

A United Methodist district superintendent tells of visiting two particular churches during his annual round of charge conferences. One was a large-membership church with a significant endowment. It also had a major physical structure that requires increasingly large financial resources to be maintained for the ministry of the church. As the church planned for a new year, it had many challenges. The superintendent wanted to support and encourage them in their efforts. He also wanted them to see that the ministry of no single congregation represents the fullness of the Christian witness. So he reminded them that they had a stake in maintaining the prophetic witness of a much smaller congregation in a small town in the district.

Not long after that, the superintendent visited the smaller church he had described to the larger congregation. They also faced significant challenges as they looked ahead to a new year of ministry. The viability of their ministry felt precarious and vulnerable because of their small size and limited financial resources. They also needed understanding and encouragement from their denominational leader and colleague. They received support. They also received a challenge to see their ministry as a part of a larger connection of Christ's witness. The superintendent reminded them that they had a stake in the ministry of the larger church in the district as it struggled to fulfill its calling in its own community. No particular expression of Christ's ministry can do everything needed for faithful mission. Likewise, no part of Christ's church is sufficient to do all that it can do without the mutual support, encouragement, and wisdom of other parts of the church.

Leaders in the Wesleyan spirit have referred to this as "the connectional principle." Connection is one of the rich concepts of the Wesleyan tradition. It is also a term we revere more than heed. It is invoked more than understood. It calls forth more honor—or, in some cases, denigration—than power.

A Theological Concept First

Part of the dilemma stems from the ways in which the common understanding and use of the term "connection" have changed. It is unfortunate that, for most American United Methodists, connection has come to mean bureaucratic connection or denominational networking. "It is a tragedy," Dennis Campbell asserts, "that the great Wesleyan theological idea of connection has been reduced to describing a system of finance, personnel, and governance." He is right that "what is at stake is nothing less than the nature and purpose of the church. Connection is first of all a theological idea."[1]

Recovering the theological meaning of connection is an important first step in recovering its power and relevance. For Wesley, connection was an ecclesiological claim. It meant that the church is not whole in any one particularity but in connection. It is not synonymous with denominational structure. Instead, it is, in Campbell's words, "a living organism of persons committed to Christ, and bound together in discipline, and under authority, for the proclamation of the gospel, and the advancement of God's reign."[2]

CONNECTION THROUGH HISTORY

Recovering a better understanding of connection in early American Methodism is a crucial next step in renewing connection. Russell Richey carefully details the nature of connection in the first days of the American church. Methodism, he notes, was not local-church-centered in the way we think of that today. The focus on the local church came more than a century later. So connection could not, in that situation, be understood as a connection of local churches.[3] There has not been in the Wesleyan tradition, according to Richey, a "morphological fundamentalism"; there has not been a fundamentalism of the local church.

The "preaching houses" were just that, places where preaching took place. Even in the 1840s and beyond, after Methodism became the largest of the denominations, thousands of Methodist preachers still preached each week without a "church building."

There was clearly a strong local expression of the faith. But, as Richey notes, "Methodist life was too dynamic, lay-centered and cooperative to be cooped up within congregations." Other words historians use to describe this early connection are missional, flexible, adaptive, expansive, pluraform, and decentralized.[4] This hardly sounds like connection as the typical layperson or clergy thinks about it today.

Richey goes on to point out that such a decentralized movement could and did embrace "black and white, rich and poor, male and female, English- and German-speaking."[5]

This was before the "pilgrimage to respectability."

MULTIFACETED EXPRESSIONS OF CONNECTION

It is indeed unfortunate that, for many today, connection has a reduced scope. Conventional thinking often reflects little more than apportionments and a series of boards and agencies.[6] It is true that a united and coordinated funding plan has been a part of connection since early in our history. Also, institutionalized ways to express a united outreach are clearly in the spirit of connectionalism. Yet connectionalism is far more multifaceted than these or any other narrow definitions acknowledge.

Russell Richey has captured the many-faceted richness of connectionalism in the Wesleyan tradition in eight concepts:

1. Connectionalism is Wesleyan; its origins have rootage in Wesley's own theology and practice.

2. Connectionalism is a distinctive and multifaceted ecclesial vision including spirituality, unity, mission, governance, and fellowship.

3. Connectionalism is a missional principle symbolized most vividly, though not exclusively, in an itinerant clergy sent where most needed.

4. Connectionalism is a covenantal commitment of faithfulness to God and accountability to the community of faith.

5. Connectionalism is an ethic of equity reflected, for example, in proportional financial support for shared ministry.

6. Connectionalism is an effective ministry delivery system that worked, especially in early America, to connect the gospel with need.

7. Connectionalism is an elastic and evolving standard that expresses itself differently in different times.

8. Connectionalism is a practical, experimental theology, a way of living our theology.[7]

NOT CONNECTION VERSUS LOCAL CHURCH

All this helps us to see that the debate today, when defined as connection versus local church, misses the historical context. What is being proposed by some is an institutionalized congregationalism to replace the corporate or bureaucratic model that has emerged over many years.

The choices of a denomination-focused connectionalism versus a local-church-focused congregationalism do not fit our Wesleyan heritage. Even a local-church-focused connectionalism does not capture the theological and historical richness of connection. What contributes more is a third alternative of a renewed connection. Or perhaps "a rediscovered connection" says it better. We do not need a new connectionalism that is merely an old congregationalism. Despite some appealing features of congregationalism, Wesleyan Christians know its limits all too well. Surely we do not need to maintain the status quo either.

Richey names the question correctly in asking where Methodism will be "at home." Will it be at home in its buildings, under corporate management, controlled by pastors? Will programming come from only one center, hemmed in by bureaucratic procedure, preoccupied with accountability? Or will Methodism reenter the homes of its people, and more important, the people who need to hear its message? Will it move out of its buildings into its neighborhoods? Will it become again too dynamic, lay-centered, and cooperative to be cooped up within a congregation? Will it reclaim a vision of church that is missional, flexible, expansive, and decentralized?[8]

The need is not a new connectionalism but the old (truly old) connectionalism of our origins. The mechanics and forms of the earlier connectionalism are not needed. But the church desperately needs the spirit of those movement days of power and transformation.

RECONNECTING METHODISM

"Our task at the end of the twentieth, and the beginning of the twenty-first century," says Dennis Campbell, "is

reconnecting Methodism."[9] Connection is constitutive of
Wesleyan Methodism. The task is to recover the richness
that goes well beyond structural questions. Such a renewed
connectionalism may be at the heart of a renewed
Wesleyan witness in the twenty-first century.

The Wesleyan connectional principle brings together self,
faith community, and society in a marvelous synergistic and
redeeming way. This dynamic, living, synergistic set of connections and relationships designed to "spread scriptural
holiness" and "reform the continent" became finally, in the
words of Gregory Schneider, "both domesticated and
bureaucratized."[10] Leaders today are called to rediscover
those living relationships.

One essential part of "reconnecting Methodism" is to find
ways to connect components of the church again in a
wholesome and life-giving way and also to connect far
more intractable divisions. How can Wesleyan Christians
become agents for connecting individuals and groups so
separated from God and one another? The Wesleyan connectional principle has always linked mission and need.
The very preoccupation with questions of "denomination
versus local church" highlights the self-preoccupation of the
church. The key question is how the power of God
revealed in Christ connects to the needs all around.

Leaders in this understanding of connection are those
who enable connection and linkage to take place. This is
far more than networking. Networking is an important
aspect; people today very much want to network to learn
and to meet needs. But connection goes further. Today's
connection will be far riskier. Christians desperately need to
name and address the increasing divisions that take away
from God's reign among people.

John Gardner's description of a "separation of the elites"
(see chapter 4) names one type of division. The urban/sub-
urban/rural differences represent another dilemma. Racial

separation, alienation, and outright racism continue to plague our life together. Age divisions will continue to be with us. The widening of the gap between the poor and the prosperous is accelerating. Can the church be a part of the answer to such division? Perhaps. Unfortunately, many churches today provide more exaggerated examples of these divisions than society as a whole does.

GLOBAL MISSION THAT EMPOWERS LOCAL DIVERSITY

As we noted earlier, it is unfortunate that "connection" has become so associated with a negative understanding of bureaucracy. It is important to remember that the bureaucracy associated with almost all large organizations today emerged almost a century ago. It was, as Rosabeth Moss Kanter points out, a very progressive development. The intent was to replace individual authoritarian leaders acting on whim or personal desire with professionals guided by fair and impartial standards. It was rational and efficient. "It was also," Kanter goes on to say, "passionless. Bureaucracy was designed for repetition, not innovation; for control, not creativity."[11]

Before a wholesale dismantling of bureaucracy takes place, we would do well to recall the positive motivations that gave rise to bureaucracy and the purposes it has served through the years. However, the times do call for ways of working that are much more dynamic, flexible, and responsive. Kanter finds the alternative to bureaucracy in a paradox. The challenge is "to think small" but, at the same time, "unite and integrate for power and scope."[12] There is a need to link the entrepreneurial spirit and approach with the connectional spirit and practices.

Other large organizations have learned that they "cannot afford a centralized bureaucracy because they lose access to essential markets" and constituencies that require local expressions and responsiveness. On the other hand, they "cannot remain a disconnected system of geographically scattered operations." The answer that many have found is what Kanter describes in an intriguing concept: "They integrate by establishing a global mission that embraces local diversity."[13]

LIVING OUR WAY INTO A NEW WAY OF THINKING

This approach is not so much a program for renewal as a theological understanding of how the church lives its life so that renewal will happen on the way. This is not a process of getting the right ideas or structures that will lead to renewal. It is the other way around. In "global mission that embraces local diversity," we engage together in common tasks, and then the programs and structures naturally follow out of the power of what God is doing.

People often ask if a new vision tends to come from the "bottom" or the "top." The best answer I know is that it does not matter—if the vision is right. However, in the case of denominational renewal in our time, answers may have to come from the "bottom." Future directions may come from people discovering clues about God's living edges in their particular places. This statement does not come from an ideological stance. It arises simply from observation and experience.

As much as all of us want a new vision for the church, that vision may not come from deliberations, no matter how wise, faithful, representative, or numerous the participants. This may be an era in which we will have to *live* our way into a new vision instead of our natural tendency to *think* our way. People more easily live their way into a new way of thinking than think their way into a new way of living. We have been trying desperately and agonizingly to think our way into a new way of living for years now. It has not worked. Everyone is weary and frustrated from the process. In this disillusionment, unproductive energy goes to casting blame.

Historically the theory of connectionalism never matched perfectly with its practice. This inconsistency does not indicate a lack of integrity so much as human limitations. While most of us can talk (theory) better than we act (practice), some claim that early Methodists did just the opposite. They often functioned day by day better than they were able to describe what it was they were doing. Such may need to become the case again. The careful rationality of our education may not always serve us well. This is particularly true as we seek to move into uncharted territories of mission. The preoccupation with getting the theory perfect and allowing no room for rough edges may prevent the release of new missional energy in a new time.

MISSION, VISION, AND RELATIONSHIPS

Connectionalism cannot survive as merely an organizational or financial concept. Connection lives when it recovers its theological rootage and foundation. There can be no true Wesleyan connection apart from mission. Mission was fundamental to the idea of connectionalism, according to Heitzenrater. Connectionalism "provided a centralized and united framework for developing and effecting a common mission."[14]

A Wesleyan connection holds together around a commitment to do what God has called the church to do. The connection gains energy by knowing that together we are engaged in the vision God has for the church in the world today. Knowing one's connection to other Christians in pursuit of God's calling for a particular time makes united efforts not only possible but essential. Every part of Christ's witness throughout the church's connection is bound together, not by obligation or tradition, but by a passion to fulfill God's will most effectively and completely.

Connection is built on mission and vision but thrives through relationships within the Christian community. As Margaret Wheatley and others have reminded us, "relationships are everything." Wesleyan connection is not an organizational chart; it is a complex set of enriching relationships among Christians. It was out of relationships formed for spiritual growth and missional outreach that virtually all the structures of today's church arose. No amount of training or literature can replace the fulfillment that comes from experiencing the bonds of Christian connection through personal and group relationships across all barriers. Such relationships were distinctive marks of early Wesleyan connection.

The connectional forms of today will change. They must change just as they have in all transition times from the beginning of the Wesleyan movement. Limitations of old forms must give way to new and innovative expressions of the connectional principle. Simply dismantling what connection has become over the years will not by itself release the power of God present in the connectional spirit. Reaffirming the mission of the church and discerning God's vision for today are essential. So too is rediscovering the relational connections—with God, other Christians, and the world. Indeed, we will do well to remember Rosabeth Moss Kanter's observation that "when bureaucracy dwindles, the quality of relationships" among people grows in importance.[15] A renewed Wesleyan connection built around mission, vision, and relationships can indeed lead to spiritual renewal.

—PART THREE—

PASSIONS OF LEADERSHIP IN THE WESLEYAN SPIRIT

CHAPTER TEN
Knows God

[The wise person's] soul is athirst for nothing on earth, but only for God, the living God.

—*John Wesley*[1]

Christian leaders would do well to reread regularly Richard Baxter's classic on pastoral leadership. *The Reformed Pastor* was first published in 1656. While Baxter had significant limitations, one knowledgeable observer said that he was "the most outstanding pastor . . . that Puritanism produced." In American Methodism, Francis Asbury used the book extensively in the training of pastors. The book so moved Asbury that he wrote in his diary on August 19, 1810, "O what a prize: Baxter's Reformed Pastor fell into my hands this morning."[2]

By "reformed," Baxter refers not to a doctrinal stance but rather to "renewal"—the renewed pastor. Baxter believed that "If God would but reform the ministry and set them on their duties zealously and faithfully, the people would certainly be reformed. All churches either rise or fall as the ministry doth rise or fall (not in riches or worldly grandeur) but in knowledge, zeal and ability for their work." Baxter maintained that Christian leaders must always take care of themselves spiritually before they can be in a position to offer help to anyone else. "Take heed . . . lest you famish yourselves while you prepare food [for others]." He continues, "Take heed, therefore, to yourselves first, that you may be that which you persuade your hearers to be and believe that which you persuade them to believe." John Wesley said it this way: "Pray . . . that, after I have preached to others, I may not myself be a castaway."[3]

What Baxter makes clear in this book written for clergy leaders of the church, we know to be true for all Christian leaders. No faithful Christian witness is possible apart from a lively and ongoing experience of God's presence in our lives. It is from this communion with God's spirit that our spirits find direction, purpose, power, and resilience.

On many occasions Wesley articulately reminded listeners of the purpose for each of us. In his sermon, "The Circumcision of the Heart," he said:

> Have no end, no ultimate end, but God.
>
> Desire not to live but to praise [God's] name: let all your thoughts, words, and works tend to [God's] glory. Set your heart firm on [God], and on other things only as they are in and from [God].[4]

Those of us seeking to serve God as leaders in the Wesleyan spirit will draw strength and guidance, as Wesley did, from Romans 12:1-2: "I appeal to you therefore, brothers and sisters, by the mercies of God, to present your bodies as a living sacrifice, holy and acceptable to God, which is your spiritual worship. Do not be conformed to this world, but be transformed by the renewing of your minds, so that you may discern what is the will of God—what is good and acceptable and perfect."

Christian leadership has to do not with our need for fulfillment but rather with God's need for vehicles to effect God's redemption in the world. Clear and focused leadership by clergy and laity is as essential today as in the first century.

Will Campbell, that eccentric Baptist preacher who defies

all attempts to stereotype him, tells of a ministry he had with a woman named Millie. She was thirty-five years old and dying of cancer in a hospital in Nashville. She claimed to be an atheist, but spent all of her energy condemning this God that did not exist. After he had visited with her over a period of several months, she said to him one day, "You know, Reverend, I just might join your church." "I don't have a church," Campbell said. After a long pause, she said, "No. I guess not. You don't have a church. A church has you."[5] This is what the letter to the Romans and John Wesley are talking about—being grasped by God for spiritual leadership.

For this leadership to be clear and focused, the leader must give singular attention to God. It is God's way and God's will that informs all leadership. It is at this point that the journey of leadership becomes both thrilling and terrifying. It is thrilling to experience one's life connected with the very power of life in the universe. It is terrifying because of the surprising and daunting adventures to which God has a habit of calling leaders. A prayer in the *Lutheran Book of Worship* contains a good reminder for all Christian leaders. "Lord God, you have called your servants to ventures of which we cannot see the ending, by paths as yet untrodden, through perils unknown."[6]

Leadership disconnected from God's power leaves leaders adrift. They then pursue their own agenda or mere self-fulfillment. Their efforts may be noble and upbuilding for the leader and others, but there is no enduring power from leadership disconnected from the source of power.

Therefore, leaders with the best of intentions find themselves presiding over church decline for lack of spiritual power. At times there are understandable reasons for the decline of churches or denominations. Unfortunately, the reasons behind the decline of mainline churches in the last generation have not been good reasons. Longed-for renewal will not come from more brochures, videos, or schemes. We need a change in the way we think. We need the renewal of our minds of which Paul speaks. We need a reconnection with the power of God. Without such a connection, there will not be "leadership in the Wesleyan spirit." Without such spiritual power, there is nothing we have to offer to a world searching for hope amidst despair.

Our calling as leaders is to discern God's vision for our future and the future of the church. Imagine vision as a picture of that to which God is calling us in the immediate future. Discernment of this preferred future—the good and acceptable and perfect—is a task essential for Christian leaders at all times. Paul warns against conforming to present realities. "How things are now" can never be synonymous with God's ultimate will. The present state of affairs in our lives and in the church always falls short of God's highest purposes. We must continually be working to discern God's vision for the future. We can never become content with the status quo.

Leadership and spirituality are inevitably linked. Leadership is only possible to the extent that we are able to discern a compelling and driving vision of what is good and acceptable and perfect. One cannot lead without such a vision. Such a vision can only come from closeness to God and to a community of believers. Leadership requires discernment of a better future. Leadership requires that we come to have a vision of what Langston Hughes described in a prayer as "The land that never has been yet—and yet must be."[7]

Now is a time for bold visions and bold leadership. Now is the time for leadership empowered by the Wesleyan spirit. Now is the time for leadership with the power that comes from the Wesleyan passion for God and God's people. Now is a time for the adventuresome leadership that most of us have known more from history books than personal experience. It is a time "to present your bodies as a living sacrifice." Or, as Letty M. Russell translates this passage, a time to "put your bodies on the line."[8]

The transforming power of leadership does not come from great wisdom or complexity. The route to God's wisdom is far more humble and simple. To renew our minds is not to separate from others or to make the simple complex. It is to "discern what is the will of God." John Wesley, in commenting on this passage, said, ". . . a Christian acts in all things by the highest reason, from the mercy of God inferring his own duty."[9]

It sounds simple. The results are far from simple. Lives change and communities experience redemption when persons identify their lives with God's will.

Robert Coles, a child psychiatrist, social critic, and Harvard professor, writes extensively about the moral life of children. A young child changed his life and the direction of his professional development. In 1960 Ruby Bridges was a six-year-old African American child, the daughter of impoverished, illiterate parents. In that year she desegregated the schools of New Orleans. Twice a day, accompanied by federal marshals, she steadily threaded her way through jeering, hateful mobs to go to school.

Coles, as he later described himself, was at that time an "arrogant young psychiatrist." He sought out Ruby Bridges. He was certain that he "could identify a psychological condition" to explain her actions. After getting to know Ruby Bridges, he said, "I could not have been more wrong." What he discovered was not a complex psychological reason for what she was doing. He found, instead, "a six-year-old's commitment to live what she had learned in the Bible."[10]

Over twenty years ago a young white pastor went to a small-town United Methodist Church in a remote and rural area of Mississippi. He had recently graduated from a very conservative seminary. The people in the church gave him a warm welcome. They anticipated with excitement the prospect of having a break from pastors who were "reformers" and "do-gooders."

As they worshiped that first summer with the new pastor's leadership, they sang all the familiar gospel songs. His sermons overflowed with "Jesus, Jesus, Jesus," pronounced in just the way they liked. Then came September when the schools opened. In that community, which was 75% African American and 25% white, all the white students were in a private school. All the African American students attended public school. Their new pastor and his wife enrolled their first-grade child as the only white student in the public school.

Soon a delegation of church members came to see the pastor. They asked why he had violated this social custom. His response was simple, reminiscent of Ruby Bridges, "This is what Jesus would have me do."

Phillips Brooks, during his first days at seminary, noticed in the dormitory some students who met regularly for a prayer meeting. Their piety impressed him. His devotional experience before coming to seminary had not included such prayer groups. Then he noticed after a few days that some of these students were among those who regularly came to class unprepared. His comment was, "The boiler had no connection with the engine."

Perhaps we have lost spiritual power today because we have cut ourselves off from the source of power, from the message that energizes. Those of us in the Wesleyan tradition love to talk about the warmed heart. Perhaps we have forgotten the fire that warmed it in the first place. "Why are we not more holy?" was one of the questions in the *Large Minutes* from the early years of Methodism. The answer was that people were "looking for the end, without using the means."

Surely the crisis of leadership in the life of the church is, at least in part, a crisis in the life of the spirit among our leaders, among ourselves. What a time for spiritual leaders with bold visions. What a time "to present your bodies as a living sacrifice." What a time to "put your bodies on the line." What a time for a new Wesleyan revival. What a time for reform of the continent. What a time for spreading scriptural holiness across the land.

A seminary president tells of a class in which one of the texts focused on the admirable goal of being responsive to the people who attend church. Apparently this particular author had gotten a bit carried away with the implications of this idea. The book suggested that the Sunday morning social time should offer at least four kinds of coffee. A Nigerian student in the class found the suggestion absurd. He did not understand all the fuss about coffee. In his country, he pointed out, people often will have walked twenty miles in order to get to church. "When they finally arrive," he said, "they are not looking for coffee. They are looking for something much more life-changing than that."

The challenge begins with church leaders. The beginning, middle, and end of all we do must emerge from seeking to know God, to discern God's calling for our time, and to do God's will. "God is not an afterthought," William McKinney reminds us. He calls mainline churches to reclaim their religious message. When so many local churches and denominations are preoccupied with their own needs and agendas, they ignore the spiritual crisis all around, or leave it to others. "If I were to criticize religious leaders today," McKinney says, "it is for our public silence on these matters of the spirit." To a large extent the rise of so many alternative sources of spiritual guidance is a reflection that other groups are doing a better job of addressing the religious needs of our neighbors.[11]

The Lutheran prayer used earlier refers to the risky nature of the calling of God. "Give us faith," it concludes, "to go out with good courage, not knowing where we go, but only that your hand is leading us and your love supporting us; through Jesus Christ our Lord."[12] It is with this confidence that we seek to become faithful, true, and great leaders in the Wesleyan spirit for the church of God.

CHAPTER ELEVEN
Proclaims Christ

It is our part thus to "preach Christ" by preaching all things whatsoever he hath revealed.

—*John Wesley*[1]

I sing by faith, pray by faith,
and do every thing by faith;
without faith in Jesus Christ
I can do nothing.

—*Harry Hoosier*[2]

Leadership in the Wesleyan spirit always remembers that for which it exists—the proclamation of Jesus Christ.

Paul's words to the Corinthian church sound strange to educated and sophisticated church leaders today. Paul speaks of the destruction of the "wisdom of the wise" and the thwarting of the "discernment of the discerning" (1 Corinthians 1:19). "God's foolishness is wiser than human wisdom, and God's weakness is stronger than human strength" (1:25). "God chose what is foolish in the world to shame the wise; God chose what is weak in the world to shame the strong" (1:27).

Should not God's people pursue wisdom? Should not they desire discernment? Should not they seek strength for their leadership in the church? Of course. But Paul's words are a reminder of how easily wisdom can become foolishness and strength, weakness. They remind us of how quickly the wisest have no truth to offer and what seems so strong loses its power. This happens when we forget what is primary. The first question of leadership is always a spiritual question of primacy. Deciding that to which the heart clings most dearly will shape what follows. Remembering what is primary will sustain leadership. Forgetting leads to foolishness and weakness.

Warren Bennis tells of a large and prestigious hospital with a new administrator. This large hospital with a budget of almost a billion dollars surprised many by selecting an academic to be its leader. He had not administered anything more complex than a committee meeting at Harvard. In addition, he was an Irish Catholic going to a Jewish hospital.

The complexity almost overwhelmed the new leader at first. There were so many claims on him and his time. Day after day he met with people and heard the issues important to them. While he had not been a formal leader before, he had the right instincts for leadership. He knew he needed the right question to focus on the primary task of the hospital.

He concluded that the purpose of the hospital was to make people well or better. Yet no one came to him with issues framed around that purpose. So, he began to ask one question about virtually everything that came to him: "How does this relate to making people well or better?" This was primary. His view was that everything else is commentary.

Wesley never forgot what was primary. Proclaiming the Good News revealed in Jesus Christ was the beginning, middle, and end of his entire life's work. He reminded others of this passion repeatedly.

You have nothing to do but to save souls. Therefore spend and be spent in this work.[3]

It is not your business to preach so many times, and to take care of this or that society; but to save as many souls as you can; to bring as many sinners as you possibly can to repentance, and with all your power to build them up in that holiness without which they cannot see the Lord.[4]

Use all the sense, learning, and time you have; forgetting yourself, and remembering only, those are the souls for whom Christ died; heirs of a happy or miserable eternity![5]

It is easy to forget the primary and focus exclusively on the commentary. This may be a major part of the dilemma for many churches today. The problem is not people's lack of interest in God. People care deeply about the purpose of life. Humanity is desperate for release from all the bondages that enslave people today. People care deeply about precisely what is primary in the Christian message. But they do not show interest in what is happening in many churches.

Just at a time when there is such a tremendous interest in religious and spiritual matters, many religious leaders and churches have no word for these spiritual needs. This is one reason people take seriously such distressing alternatives: religious leaders have left a vacuum. It is into this vacuum, for example, that a generic spirituality moves which is grounded in nothing more than self-centeredness.

"We need to reclaim a new assertiveness regarding the religious message," says William McKinney, "particularly because established churches in the U.S. are failing to address our country's spiritual crisis."[6]

While many denominations talk about fewer churches and fewer members, there are actually more churches today than ever and more people searching for purpose, meaning, and hope for their lives. If these people are not in our churches, it may be a reflection of McKinney's observation that other groups are simply doing a better job of addressing the religious needs of our neighbors.[7]

Paul's words also remind us of the need for a new humility. "So let no one boast about human leaders" (1 Corinthians 3:21*a*). This boasting in human leaders is precisely what the Corinthians, in their party conflicts, had been doing. One boasted in Paul, another in Apollos, another in Cephas. This mistakes the relationship between the Christian and the leader, according to C. K. Barrett. It inverts the truth.[8]

Christians do not belong to their leaders (or parties, theologies, or politics). All things, including these things and more, belong to Christians. Indeed, the world, life, death, things present, and things to come all belong to the Christian. And Christians belong to Christ (1 Corinthians 3:21*b*-23).

What then about Paul, Apollos, and Cephas? What then about my favorite theologian or my special social cause? They remain important. But no leader or ideology ever can be a lord over God's people. No person or perspective can be a lord before whom God's people bow. Everything stands evaluated in relationship to what is primary—Jesus Christ.

When we forget this lesson, we are in trouble. Tom Long contends that this loss of the power of purpose has had a severe impact upon denominations. In so many denominations in the U.S. today, he says, we are "beating each other over the head on issues precisely because we do not expect anything to happen. We have no eschatology. We have no hope." He goes on to say that what we have left is the institution. "And when all you have is the institution," he maintains, "you start dividing up the turf theologically, financially, and in terms of power committing acts of violence."[9]

Instead of placing ourselves as religious leaders in the

middle of the poor, the lost, the neglected, the vulnerable, and those searching for meaning and hope for their despair, we have placed ourselves in the middle of an elitist culture war. In this war the church is no more than, as Peter Schmiechen puts it, "another arm of ideological conflict."[10]

Thus, the church has no real message. The gospel message is not a message of debate. God's proclaimers are not the debaters of this age. Instead, the Christian message is a "go and tell" message. Jesus said to the disciples, "Go and tell John what you have seen and heard: the blind receive their sight, the lame walk, the lepers are cleansed, the deaf hear, the dead are raised, the poor have good news brought to them" (Luke 7:22).

At the very time we need to proclaim, "Behold the Lamb of God that taketh away the sin of the world," we want to argue instead. Just when we need to say, "Where sin abounded, grace did much more abound," we want to condemn.

There is a new fundamentalism today. It is in every church, every denomination, every seminary. For some this new fundamentalism is built around doctrine. For others it is a fundamentalism of moral behavior. For still others the fundamentalism centers on social positions. In all this certainty, what becomes lost is the reality that all of us—no matter how true our doctrine, how spotless our moral behavior, or how pure our social principles—are in need of God's grace and love, as well as judgment and forgiveness for all our human limitations.

When Paul reminds us of the primacy of Christ and the cross, notice the wording. "For the message about the cross is foolishness to those who are perishing, but to us who are being saved it is the power of God" (1 Corinthians 1:18). If there is a need for a greater assertiveness about the primacy of Jesus Christ, there is also a need for a greater humility that comes from knowing we are all being saved.

What a reminder this is for church life today. Our wisdom and discernment are important but not enough. In worship it is important to pronounce words correctly rather than to mispronounce. It is better to sing appropriate hymns for appropriate seasons of the year than not to do so. It is better to use inclusive language than exclusive language. It is better to interpret scripture carefully than casually. It is better for our theology to be consistent than inconsistent. However, in the world of today most people care little about what matters to us theologically, liturgically, and socially, unless we have been agents of God's love for their lives. Have they experienced the forgiveness of sins through Christ? Are they reconciled with others? Have they connected with the very power of God? Have they given their lives to Jesus Christ?

When we forget what is primary, religious leaders become like the false shepherds described in Ezekiel 34 who feed themselves but not the sheep. "You eat the fat, you clothe yourselves with the wool, you slaughter the fatlings; but you do not feed the sheep. You have not strengthened the weak, you have not healed the sick, you have not bound up the injured, you have not brought back the strayed, you have not sought the lost, but with force and harshness you have ruled them" (vv. 3-4). The sheep became scattered because they had no real shepherd.

God's leaders seek wisdom. They pray always for discernment. They nurture strength for the journey. They study. They seek to be true in their doctrine, lives, and social commitments. Yet God's true leaders also know that all of this will be but foolishness if leaders are not good shepherds of all of God's people.

The good shepherd is the one who will seek the lost, bring back the strayed, bind up the injured, and strengthen the weak (Ezekiel 34:16).

And, if there is success? If pews are full, the blind see,

the lame walk, those who hate come to love, and those who make war become lovers of peace, then God's leaders never boast in themselves. They heed Paul's advice, "Let the one who boasts, boast in the Lord" (1 Corinthians 1:31).

There are many ways to understand the history of the Methodist movement. Some focus on the personalities of key leaders while others point to decisive historical events and turning points. Still others highlight polity and specifically the impact of an itinerant "sent" ministry on early Methodism in America. While there are many reasonable windows through which to understand Methodism, the dimension that gives meaning to them all is *the message* of the Wesleyan movement.

Albert Outler reminds us what was crucial from the very beginning of the Wesleyan Revival: "Wesley's message . . . counted for more than his manner." "There are only occasional flights of eloquence" in his preaching, he contends. "Wesley's message is Wesley's medium."[11]

James Logan acknowledges that Wesley's personality and organizational ability were important factors in the Wesleyan revival. Yet he maintains that "the great power of the revival was inherent in its message and, above all, in the Person whom the message bore witness." The Wesleyan message was always key. "One can hardly underestimate," says Logan, "the powerful attraction of the message of universal grace." While the Wesleyan message was "plain truth for plain people," it was not a simplistic message. The Wesleyan "witness to the gospel was a rugged message of divine grace."[12]

The first question asked at the Christmas Conference in Baltimore in 1784 was "For what are we here?" The specific wording was "What may we reasonably believe to be God's design in raising up the preachers called Methodists?"

Their answer—"to reform the continent and spread scriptural holiness throughout the land."

One does not have to oversimplify or romanticize the past to say that there was a clear and commonly shared focus; stated most succinctly, they would probably have put it, "to save souls."

John Wesley had a burning desire for all humanity to come to know the love of God revealed in Jesus Christ. This was his overriding passion. It was his paramount concern. It was at the heart of his life's work. There is no way to understand Wesley or early Methodism apart from this guiding vision.

Phillips Brooks reflected this spirit of Wesley as he addressed students at Yale Divinity School years ago in his Lyman Beecher Lectures. He exhorted: "Preach doctrine, preach all the doctrine you know, and learn forever more and more; but preach it always, not that [people] may believe it, but that [people] may be saved by believing it."

A strong case exists that we have forgotten that for which we are here. I am not talking about mimicking past language, understandings, or concepts. Rather, we do not have a common shared vision that comes from the core of why the church exists and what it means to be a people called United Methodists.

The good news is that, as Walter Brueggemann has reminded us, "forgetters can become rememberers. . . . Evangelism is a task not simply of making outsiders into insiders, but of summoning insiders from amnesia to memory." It is this amnesia, which is "massive among us," that explains the lack of "any serious missional energy. It is only this odd memory . . . that gives energy for social action, generosity in stewardship, freedom for worship, courage in care for outsiders, and passion for God's promises."[13]

Brueggemann also reminds us that "the noun 'gospel,' which means 'message,' is linked in the Bible to the verb 'tell-the-news.' . . . At the center of the act of evangelism is the message announced. . . . There is no way that anyone, including an embarrassed liberal, can avoid this lean, decisive assertion which is at the core of evangelism."[14]

In ways that Wesley would appreciate, Brueggemann also reminds us that the act of announcement occurs within a context requiring serious attention. "No reductionist conservative can faithfully treat evangelism as though it were only 'naming the name.' " What follows the proclamation is "the difficult, demanding work of reordering all of life according to the claim of the proclaimed verdict."[15]

Some would contend that a common, shared vision similar to that of early American Methodism is no longer possible in the contemporary United Methodist Church because of all the diversity today. If that is the case, and I hope it is not, then the prospects are not bright for the church. Short of a renewed common vision, organizations tend either to flounder and decline or to divide into a number of smaller more focused entities. Neither option represents the best of the Wesleyan heritage.

No organization can ever be strong unless there is a common, unifying, shared vision that is stronger than any of the differences that divide. For that reason we need always to be searching for the one thing that is at the center, that guides everything else and gives meaning and direction to all that we do. A major part of the loss of organizational memory involves forgetting that for which we exist. The words of Jesus to Martha speak to the heart of our predicament—"You are fretting and fussing about so many things; but [only] one thing is necessary" (Luke 10:41-42 NEB).

In seeking the one thing that will guide us into the future, we are called to reclaim our Wesleyan heritage. We need to remember that the first task for Wesley was always evangelism.

Georgia Harkness years ago reflected both the dilemma and hope of the churches in a way that sounds remarkably contemporary on both counts. "What then ails our churches?" she asked. "Inadequate numbers, unhealthy divisions, meager financial support, unprophetic leadership, lethargic congregations—all these and many more symptoms of ill health are found. But at the root of them all lies the fact that the very thing for which the Church exists—the proclamation of the gospel—is being in our time so feebly done."[16]

Harkness is right that the powerful communication of the gospel is "the most important task under God that any person can undertake."[17] Many of our debates today would seem strange to those who have gone before us in the Wesleyan heritage. Our debates over personal faith versus social gospel, while recognizable, would be hard for them to understand. However, what would be many times more difficult for them to understand is the questioning of the priority of the evangelical call to share the good news with those outside the faith community. What would be impossible for them to understand would be the questioning of evangelism as the priority for every church and for every leader in the church.

An incident at a continuing education event highlighted this need for remembering our primary message of proclaiming Christ. Bill Cotton, a United Methodist pastor in Iowa, finished a presentation to a group made up mostly of clergy. He had given a ringing call for churches to take on the principalities and powers that dominate our lives and communities. At the same time, he called upon pastors to lead in "growing churches" by sharing the good news with those outside their walls. During the question time someone said, "When you talk about growing churches, aren't you going back to that old numbers game?" There was a stunned look of disbelief on Bill's face. His response was, "I have never understood inviting someone to the Lord's table as anything other than what I was called to do."

Some people say numbers are not important. It is true

that numbers are not important for most of us—unless they happen to deal with something that matters greatly to us. When the issue at stake is important, then numbers become important to us. Have you ever had the experience of being in a meeting where an issue close to the hearts of the participants is under discussion? Numbers and percentages receive close attention, compared year by year and decade by decade. In that setting, to question this careful attention to numbers would not make sense. It is not enough to say that the focus should be on intent, quality, or some other nonobjective categories. Such an argument will normally elicit a response something like: "We need to look at the numbers because there is a difference in intent and impact." And they are right to monitor the numbers.

One then goes into another meeting where the issue is church members received by confession of faith. In that setting, for many people, to talk about numbers seriously is off-limits. The only difference between the numbers in the two meetings is that in the latter case the numbers are referring to people who have said, "Yes, I want to begin the pilgrimage of faith. Yes, I believe in Jesus Christ."

We need to hear again those words from Ephesians, I was "made a minister, by God's gift." I have been "granted . . . the privilege of proclaiming . . . the good news of the unfathomable riches of Christ" (Ephesians 3:7-8 NEB). The different translations of this verse indicate just how precious are these riches: "unsearchable riches, incalculable riches, inexhausted wealth, fathomless wealth." There is still no better way to say it than "Good News."

Recovering both the "conviction that the gospel matters, and a passionate concern for a person's relation to God" would be nothing other than reclaiming the heritage that already belongs to the mainline churches, according to Leander Keck. "If that happens," he maintains, "these churches can once more commend the gospel with confidence. And hungering and distraught people will hear again some Good News from their pulpits."[18]

NONE BUT CHRIST

Henry Evans was "a giant among the early Methodist preachers," says William B. McClain. Evans, an African American, ministered in the South as an itinerant Methodist preacher during the late 1700s and early 1800s after being converted to Christianity in his youth. He was known as an extremely gifted and effective preacher and served as a pastor for both whites and blacks. Several churches consider him as their founder.

In 1810 Evans spoke for the last time at a church he had begun, where he was living in a room attached to the chancel. The pastor at the time, a white preacher later elected bishop in the Southern church, described what happened that day:

The little door between his humble shed and the chancel where I stood was opened and the dying man entered for a last farewell to his people. He was almost too feeble to stand at all, but supporting himself by the railing of the chancel, he said: "I have come to say my last word to you. It is this: None but Christ. . . ."[19]

CHAPTER TWELVE
Seeks Justice

BIBLICAL

The Wesleyan passion for justice comes directly from the biblical witness.

Perhaps the most significant encounter in the history of the Hebrew people was God's call to Moses. We know the story well. Moses experiences the holiness of the presence of God. Then just as Moses is ready to bask in the spiritual glow of this religious experience, God calls him for a task. He is to go to the governor and lobby for better pay, improved working conditions, fair employment practices, and, yes, the liberation of an oppressed people.

Moses did not think this had anything to do with religion so he protested vigorously, arguing with God five times. Yet it was his acceptance of this mission that marked a turning point in the story of our salvation history.

Moses went to Pharaoh declaring, "Let my people go." Pharaoh felt Moses should stay out of politics.

Later came the prophets. The distinction is frequently made between false prophets and true prophets. False prophets bless the status quo and say what the rulers desire to hear. True prophets challenge cultural and social assumptions with, "Thus saith the Lord."

Amos is a good example. This country preacher saw many amazing things in the city. He found a bustling economy. He also saw persons sent to debtors' prison owing no more than the price of a pair of shoes. He saw businesspersons taking advantage of the illiterate. He observed a judicial system corrupt from local courts all the way to the "Supreme Court." He saw religion used more for the sake of its leaders than for the people.

Then he attended religious services at a leading house of worship filled with people. Amos stood to speak to this congregation. It was no speech of congratulations for their statistical success. Amos had a word from God. He said God hates all this outward show because a game is being played. "You are trying to be religious when God calls for total righteousness," was his message to them. God hates all of this unless you get your political, social, and economic house in order and "let justice roll down like waters, and righteousness like an everflowing stream" (Amos 5:24).

The greatest biblical witness comes in Jesus. From the beginning of his life he was a threat to the established and unjust political orders. It was a politician who sought to kill him shortly after his birth. It was politicians who finally succeeded in crucifying him. Jesus did not die because he talked about lilies of the field and birds in the air. He went to the cross because he talked of thieves in the marketplace, rascals in the statehouse, and a God demanding total allegiance.

HISTORICAL

From the earliest days, the Christian church has involved itself with the redemption of society as well as of individuals. Early Christians fought against the social evils of infanticide, bloody gladiatorial contests, and human slavery. Throughout history every tyrant from Nero to Hitler to contemporary dictators has sought first to silence the Christian church.

The difference among churches historically has not been that some involve themselves with social and political issues and others do not. The difference is rather the variety of issues with which they have chosen to deal. Interestingly, some churches that claim to "stay out of politics" are the first to become involved when their particular issues arise. Even churches that appear to withdraw from society (by not voting, for example) are making a significant political witness. They are giving strong support to the status quo with all of its inadequacies and limitations.

WESLEYAN EXAMPLE

John Wesley was indeed clear on the unity of faith and action. "The gospel of Christ knows of no religion, but social," he said, "no holiness but social holiness."[1] The Wesleyan Revival fostered a change of individuals and society—together. The Wesleyan movement consistently held together personal and social holiness.

Revolutionary changes in English life resulted from this movement of God. Kenneth E. Boulding said, "It was not the economists who liberated slaves or who passed the Factory Acts, but the rash and ignorant Christians." The Wesleyan movement created a social and political force in England that played a crucial role in what Wilberforce called "the revolution of manners and morals" in English society.[2]

The Wesleyan movement was first a religious revival that stressed personal religious experience. However, from the beginning of this movement, the implications of repentance for social reform received serious attention.

Virtually all denominations that share the Wesleyan tradition have shared to a greater or lesser degree this Wesleyan passion for social justice. Indeed, a number of church divisions have been related to justice issues, particularly when the church seemed to accommodate its witness to injustice. History teaches us all humility, even in the brighter chapters. No one branch of the Wesleyan witness has had a monopoly on justice. If anything, history shows how much we need to learn from one another. Righteous pride can make it harder to see one's own accommodation to injustice.

One need only look at the early Methodist involvement in England with poverty, slavery, liquor, education, and prisons to see the scope of their concern. In America the linkage between personal and social comes as early as the Christmas Conference of 1784. One action of this organizing conference called for the abolition of slavery.

LEADERSHIP AND RACISM—A MIXED HISTORY

No understanding of leadership today can avoid the issue of racism. The Wesleyan passion for justice, combined with a very mixed history in regard to racial justice, mandates such leadership.

As we have seen, African Americans were a part of the Methodist movement in America from the very beginning. At no time have African Americans been absent from the drama of the American Wesleyan witness. The response of the larger Methodist constituency to their presence has been at best a mixed history. "Beginning with the first organized Methodist Society at Sam's Creek in Frederick County, Maryland," says William B. McClain, "and continuing through the last General Conference of the United Methodist Church, is the all-too-familiar question: 'What shall we do with the blacks?' "[3]

The organizing conference of American Methodism condemned the practice of slavery. The action was bold and prophetic for the time. It called for the expulsion of any

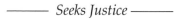

member engaging in the slave trade. However, *within a year* this strong stand began to weaken through accommodation. In 1785 Thomas Coke defended the backtracking "on account of the great opposition that had been given it, our work being in too infantile a state to push things to extremity." By early in the 1800s Methodism had largely accommodated to the institution of slavery, with only nominal official disapproval preserved. "The door to compromise on this moral issue was opened," says McClain, "and has never been securely and permanently closed from that day to this."[4]

Increasingly the Methodists came to see sin as individualized to the exclusion of more systemic expressions of sin such as racism. There were those who bravely sought to hold concerns for individual moral responsibility and corporate morality together. The movement that led to the formation of the Wesleyan Methodist Church came from a protest against Methodist accommodation to slavery. While not alone in their opposition, the Wesleyan Methodists do stand out for their efforts to link "piety and radicalism."[5]

The exclusion and mistreatment of African Americans led to the formation of the African Methodist Episcopal Church and later the African Methodist Episcopal Church, Zion, and the Christian Methodist Episcopal Church. The issue of slavery that divided America in the nineteenth century also divided Methodism into a northern church and a southern church. The price of reunion in 1939 was paid largely by African Americans with the establishment of the racially segregated Central Jurisdiction. "Of the forty-seven African American delegates to the General Conference" that year, "thirty-six voted against the Plan of Union and eleven abstained. . . . When the General Conference rose to sing, 'We Are Marching to Zion,' the African American delegates remained seated, and some of them wept."[6] The Central Jurisdiction existed for approximately thirty years.

Clearly race has "constituted one of the most fundamental challenges to Methodism." It is a challenge in which Methodism, according to Donald Dayton, has "by and large" failed the test.[7]

CHURCH AND SOCIETY FAILING THE TEST

Unfortunately, Methodism is not alone in the way it has addressed this challenge to justice. W. E. B. DuBois wrote in 1901 that the problem of the twentieth century is the problem of the color line. What prophetic words he spoke. At the end of the century there is still a color line that runs through the heart of America.

Despite this reality, for well over a century there have been premature celebrations of victories over racism. There is a real hope engendered by some progress. Such victories do lead to optimism. Yet it is the reality of our common life that illustrates the intractable nature of the sin of racism in our culture. As Gloria Yamato put it in 1992:

> Like a virus, it's hard to beat racism, because by the time you come up with a cure, it's mutated to a "new cure-resistant" form. One shot just won't get it. Racism must be attacked from many angles.[8]

Events in the United States and around the world make it clear that racism still stands as the pressing challenge for us who would be leaders of the church and society. Racism is real, alive, and no one of us can deny that reality or claim exemption from its insidious power.

A few years ago United Methodists in the United States responded to a survey asking them to name the issues they thought God was most calling the church to address. Another question asked about their optimism for success in dealing with each issue. The issue that emerged at the top of the survey was racism. It is significant that this result came from people in a denomination that is 95% white. There was an equally significant, and far more disturbing, finding. While people listed racism as highest regarding the need for attention, racism ranked lowest in terms of probability of success for dealing with it.

We see this attitude of both urgency and despair reflected in Jonathan Kozol's disturbing book about American public education, *Savage Inequalities.* He asked one New York City school administrator if he thought black and white children would ever go to school together. The administrator replied, "I don't see it." At another school, he interviewed a class of Hispanic and African American ninth graders where only one had ever gone to school with a white child. Kozol asked them how long they thought it would be before children of all races went to school together in this country. After a moment, one of the student leaders replied, "Give it another 200 years." The other students nodded in agreement.[9]

THE CHURCH'S CHALLENGE

Whatever political and social progress we have made has not always been matched by spiritual progress. Over ten years ago, speaking in the chapel of Saint Paul School of Theology, Bishop Woodie White said, "While we dismantled the racist structure, we did not dismantle the racist spirit."

As much as we may wish it to be different, the church is not immune to this deadly "virus" of racism. In addition to bringing with us the racist social conditioning of our culture, many people in mainline denominations come from communities and institutions in which they have not experienced diversity. Too many of us bring far too little experience or understanding of those who are different from us. Martin Luther King Jr. reminded us years ago that the Sunday worship hour remains the most segregated hour of the week in America.

We must acknowledge that racism has a more profound impact on the church than most of us can ever fully appreciate or understand. We must grieve every instance of hurt endured by a child of God because of words or actions based on race, no matter what the motivations or intentions. But grief is not enough. We must acknowledge and confess our shortcomings. As leaders we must also set a plan of action. Only decisive action will make the church truly an hospitable environment. The church can become a place where all are safe. The church can become a place in which all are honored as God's precious and unique creations for whom Christ died.

Racism has no place in the Christian church. It is a sin against God and everything for which the church stands. Only those who can understand and accept that we are one in Christ can be credible ambassadors for Christ in a world growing more diverse daily. Leadership in the Wesleyan spirit requires us to declare that racism is wrong, and we must work constantly to confront it and end it.

All of us as leaders—in our churches, in our communities, in our relationships, in all of our life and work—are called to recommit ourselves. Such rededication is necessary to address the monumental task of eliminating the racism among us.

The task at times appears overwhelming. Yet, despite its magnitude, God is calling this generation, through the church, to move forward in faithfulness. There is no one solution. Progress takes place when many become involved in diverse efforts for leadership by the church. We will do well to remember Dr. King's admonition that justice requires many approaches: "Anyone who starts out with the conviction that the road to racial justice is only one lane wide will inevitably create a traffic jam and make the journey infinitely longer."[10]

Andrew Young served with King and later held many high public offices. After serving as mayor of Atlanta, he ran unsuccessfully for Governor of Georgia. When he met with his supporters the last time, he talked about prejudice, not just the racial prejudice that he had experienced, but all prejudice. Then he talked about our children as the promise of the future, those who will lead us to a better day. As he finished and walked away, two young white boys were waiting to get his autograph. These were the children he was talking about—the youth, the hope of tomorrow. An observer watching this scene said, "You could not help but ask yourself, however, how many more generations we will have to go through, putting our faith in our youth because we have failed the faith that our parents' generation had put in us, when we were the youth."

Those who would be leaders in the Wesleyan spirit have a mandate to work so all may come to know healing and reconciliation in our time through the power of Christ.

"Valhalla Syndrome" or Cosmopolitan Vision

There are signs that the growing urbanization and diversity of America in the twentieth century are producing potentially destructive reactions. Joel Kotkin believes that some of the movement away from cities is a reaction to the cacophony of urban life. He calls this the "Valhalla syndrome—a yearning for a heavenly retreat, with the promised reward of a simpler, less complex existence." He predicts that the impact of the Valhalla syndrome may be even more profound in the next century. This could guarantee a growing racial and cultural chasm between "the cosmopolitan cities and the Valhallan hinterland on a scale not seen since the divisions that led to the Civil War."[11]

Like the struggle between the rural South and urbanized North of the nineteenth century, this conflict between Valhallan and cosmopolitan visions will likely shape the America of the twenty-first century. Ultimately, Kotkin warns, this struggle of visions "may determine whether the society meets the challenge of becoming a harbinger of a new world culture, or whether it will seek to freeze itself, like other declining civilizations, in the comforting outlines of its imagined past."[12]

GLOBAL TRIBES

The twentieth century began with great optimism. Reason would prevail. There indeed could be a new world order. Progress was inevitable. Many believed that the great "melting pot" effect of America would make the power of racial, ethnic, national, and religious origins decrease. The end of the twentieth century finds the opposite to be the case. There is renewed interest in all types of rootage. "Tribalism," as sociologist Harold Isaacs has said, "did not go away."[13]

For some, this development is frightening. They associate this type of new tribalism with the worst examples of warring factions in the past. It is seen as "a throwback to the basest kind of clannishness." This increased emphasis on one's own culture "often suggests the prospect of a humanity breaking itself into narrow, exclusive and often hostile groups."[14]

This new tribalism, however, may be remarkably different. Today there are what Kotkin calls "global tribes." They are forged by globally dispersed ethnic groups. They are "today's quintessential cosmopolitans, in sharp contrast to narrow provincials." As people become more dispersed and the identities of nation states become less powerful, linkages that bind together people across nations and time will become more important.[15]

Global tribes bear the traditional tribal marks of a common origin and shared values. Now those characteristics are linked with "geographic dispersion and a belief in scientific progress," according to Kotkin. Instead of surrendering their sense of distinctive ethnic identity, these global tribes "utilize their historically conditioned values and beliefs to cope successfully with change."[16]

So it is that we in the church will need to find new ways to recognize and value distinctive identities and cultures. At the same time, we may discover anew the unity which comes from "doing justice" to our diversity.

JUSTICE BELONGS TO ALL WESLEYANS

Heitzenrater finds one common thread that ran through the varied traditions that Wesley appreciated and sought to bridge—"the French Catholic mystics, the German Lutherans, the English Calvinists, the American Revivalists, and the Scottish evangelicals." That common theme is a "holistic concern for the well-being of God's creatures—mind, body, and soul."[17]

I remembered that statement about Wesley when I read these words from Reinhold Niebuhr: "Inherited dogmas and generalizations will not be accepted, no matter how revered or venerable," he said, "if they do not contribute to the establishment of justice in a given situation." This Wesleyan theme was echoed in Rebecca Chopp's book about theological education. In *Saving Work* she describes justice as constitutive of the church rather than something distributed by the church through charity. She contends that justice, in a sense, "defines the mission and nature of the ekklesia."[18]

That statement about Wesley's "holistic concern for the well-being" of all also caused me to think about words I first read long ago. Twenty-five years ago, following a national meeting of United Methodists seeking evangelical renewal of the church, seminary professor Claude H. Thompson wrote an article presenting his hopes for evangelical renewal. He wrote as an evangelical. He also wrote as someone with high hopes for genuine Wesleyan evangelical renewal of his church. If this evangelical renewal is to become a reality, he maintained, it must surely be manifest around three issues. For Thompson the three issues were: war, poverty, and racism. His three issues are not the "hot button" issues of today. They are issues that strike the heart of the Christian and Wesleyan passion for justice.

"This is an hour when United Methodist evangelicals are called to conquest to eliminate these evils from our society," Thompson declared. "And the same motivations which drove Francis Asbury up and down the new republic of America and John Wesley all over Great Britain, must come to possess the inheritors of that dynamic."[19]

Just think how our ideological debates of the last twenty-five years might have been different if dominated by this Wesleyan concern for the mind and body and soul of all people. In the Wesleyan tradition, justice is not the property of one end of the theological spectrum. It is the shared passion of all true exemplars of the Wesleyan spirit.

CONCLUSION

Traditions, including the Wesleyan tradition, do not continue without great care and struggle. No tradition, regardless of how true or rich, is self-explanatory for new times and new challenges. Every generation of leaders in the Wesleyan tradition must discover anew the meaning of the Wesleyan legacy. That continues to be our task today.

It is true that the Wesleyan movement achieved results well beyond anything Wesley himself could have imagined. Yet the great strength of the Wesleyan legacy lies not in the successes or failures of any historical period. Rather, as Heitzenrater has put it so well, the Wesleyan heritage takes its vital energy from the "dynamic imagery of the spiritual pilgrimage." He describes this Wesleyan pilgrimage as "the story of a people struggling together to understand God and themselves as they move from birth to death, from new birth to eternal life, from fear to joy, from doubt to confidence."[1]

The great example of Wesley for future generations is not as a model leader. He was far from that. His lasting example is a spiritual legacy of one who spent virtually his entire lifetime on this same pilgrimage. Until his dying moments he continued to seek growth in grace, peace of soul, communion with God, and perfection in love.

Late in his life, an aged Wesley wrote a letter to Ellen Gretton, a pioneer Methodist preacher in England. These words also speak to us who seek to be a faithful new generation of leaders in the Wesleyan spirit:

> I trust you will find new zeal for God and new vigour in pursuing every measure which may attend to the furtherance

of [God's] kingdom. . . . Go humbly and steadily on . . . pressing on to perfection.[2]

The question facing us as contemporary heirs of the Wesleyan spirit is, "Can we create a future worthy of our past?"

Without a new vision, the future does not look bright. For example, if United Methodist membership decline continues as now during the first decade of the twenty-first century, membership as a percentage of population will drop to the same level as in the first decade of the nineteenth century. If congregations continue to look inward, the great passion for spreading scriptural holiness and reforming the nation will live only in our past.

It does not have to be that way.

My hope is that a new leadership in the Wesleyan spirit will so emerge from young and old, newcomers and veterans, that new vision and new life will result. My prayer is that as we all work together, the future will not only be worthy of the past but far more faithful than ever before.

Indeed, it is in times of hardship that new visions are likely to emerge. It was in a time of despair that Nehemiah and his people united to rebuild the wall. It was after hundreds of years of suffering that Habakkuk sought and received the vision that the just shall live by faith. In was in the midst of life-denying realities that Jesus proclaimed the vision that all might have abundant life.

Would it not be a blessing if at some future General Conference a speaker addressing the Conference would make the following statement and immediately all heads would nod in instant recognition of its truth?

As I think back on United Methodism in recent times, the only fitting description is in the words written years ago to the church at Thyatira. "I know all your ways, your love and faithfulness, your good service and your fortitude; and of late you have done even better than at first." (Revelation 2:19 NEB)

NOTES

Introduction

1. Jean Miller Schmidt, "Women's History, Everyone's History," Wertsch Lectures, Saint Paul School of Theology, 1995. She is quoting historian Donald G. Matthews's address at the "Women in New Worlds" conference held in Cincinnati, Ohio, 1980.

2. Leander E. Keck, *The Church Confident* (Nashville: Abingdon, 1993), 16.

3. Martin E. Marty, foreword to *A Conspiracy of Goodness: Contemporary Images of Christian Mission,* by Donald E. Messer (Nashville: Abingdon, 1992), 13.

1. Begins with People

1. Lillian Smith, *Killers of the Dream,* rev. ed. (New York: Anchor, 1963), 85.

2. Nathan O. Hatch, *The Democratization of American Christianity* (New Haven: Yale University Press, 1989), 127. Hatch is writing about the Wesleyan impact on the American religious experience.

3. Thomas Haweis, *An Impartial and Succinct History of the Rise and Declension and Revival of the Church of Christ* (London, 1807), 2:435-36, quoted in Albert C. Outler, *John Wesley's Sermons: An Introduction* (Nashville: Abingdon, 1991), 18.

4. Barbara Brown Taylor, *When God Is Silent* (Cambridge, Mass.: Cowley, 1998), 93, 98.

5. William Warren Sweet, *Religion on the American Frontier, 1783–1840,* vol. 4, *The Methodists* (Chicago: University of Chicago Press, 1946), 51.

6. Hatch, *Democratization,* 127.

7. Mary Parker Follett, *The New State* (New York: Longmans, Green and Company, 1923), 218.

8. Robert Wuthnow, *The Crisis in the Churches: Spiritual Malaise, Fiscal Woe* (New York: Oxford University Press, 1997), 5.

9. C. Kirk Hadaway and David A. Roozen, *Rerouting the Protestant Mainstream: Sources of Growth and Opportunities for Change* (Nashville: Abingdon, 1995), 35.

2. Follows the People

1. Nathan O. Hatch, *The Democratization of American Christianity* (New Haven: Yale University Press, 1989), p. 89.

2. Carl Bangs, "The Strangeness of American Methodism: An Essay in Historical Theology," a lecture at Saint Paul School of Theology, April 2, 1998.

3. Hatch, *Democratization,* 89.

Notes to pages 23-37

4. While predominant, this attitude was by no means unanimous. "For Methodist itinerants, the growth of the port towns in the new republic posed a special challenge. Not all Methodists assumed, like Asbury, that cities were places where Methodism could not thrive, or that farming folk would find its message more appealing." Doris Elisabeth Andrews, "Popular Religion and the Revolution in the Middle Atlantic Ports: The Rise of the Methodists, 1770–1800" (Ph.D. diss., University of Pennsylvania, 1986), 270.

5. William Henry Williams, *The Garden of American Methodism: The Delmarva Peninsula, 1769–1820* (Wilmington, Del.: Scholarly Resources, 1984), 91-92.

6. *Western Christian Advocate*, 6 January 1843, quoted in D. R. McAnally, *History of Methodism in Missouri* (St. Louis: Advocate Publishing House, 1881), 1:173.

7. The percentage remained close to this figure from 1850 to 1950 with some fluctuation within those years.

8. Doris Kearns Goodwin, *No Ordinary Time: Franklin and Eleanor Roosevelt: The Home Front in World War II* (New York: Simon & Schuster, 1994), 43, 624.

9. Sam Roberts, *Who We Are: A Portrait of America Based on the Latest U.S. Census,* rev. ed. (New York: Times Books, 1995), 9, 116.

10. Ibid., 9.

11. Barbara Crossette, "The Return of the City-State," *New York Times,* 2 June 1996, E4.

12. Jon Margolis, "The Reopening of the Frontier," *New York Times Magazine,* 15 October 1995, 52.

13. Ibid.

14. Joel Kotkin, "In America, the Middle Class Heads for the Hills," *International Herald Tribune,* 14 March 1996.

15. There is a racial dimension to this migration. Most of the rural migration is by whites. Thus, the growing diversity of the nation is actually a diversity in parts of the nation, while other parts remain unchanged or actually less diverse. Steven A. Holmes, "Leaving the Suburbs for Rural Areas," *New York Times,* 19 October 1997.

16. Kotkin, "Middle Class Heads for the Hills."

17. David S. Broder, "Inner-City Squeeze," *Washington Post,* 26 June 1996, A21.

3. Focuses on Serving

1. William Golding, *The Spire* (London: Faber and Faber, 1964), 220.

2. Edward F. Wimberly and Anne Streaty Wimberly, quoted in James O. Stallings, *Telling the Story: Evangelism in Black Churches* (Valley Forge, Pa.: Judson, 1988), 59.

3. Maria Harris, *Fashion Me a People: Curriculum in the Church* (Louisville: Westminster/John Knox, 1989), 146.

4. Letty M. Russell, *Human Liberation in a Feminist Perspective: A Theology* (Philadelphia: Westminster, 1974), 143, 140, 142, 145. For a different perspective, see Jacquelyn Grant, "The Sin of Servanthood and the Deliverance of Discipleship," in *A Troubling in My Soul: Womanist Perspectives on Evil and Suffering,* ed. Emilie M. Townes (Maryknoll, N.Y.: Orbis, 1993), 199-218; and "Servanthood Revisited: Womanist Explorations of Servanthood Theology," in *The Papers of the Henry Luce III Fellows in Theology,* ed. Jonathan Strom (Atlanta: Scholars Press, 1997), 2:25-41.

5. Richard Bondi, *Leading God's People: Ethics for the Practice of Ministry* (Nashville: Abingdon, 1989), 41-42.

149

6. Albert C. Outler, *Evangelism in the Wesleyan Spirit* (Nashville: Tidings, 1971), 103, 104.

7. Archbishop William Temple: "It is a mistake to suppose that God is primarily interested in religion."

4. Remembers Especially the Poor

1. *The Letters of the Rev. John Wesley, A.M.,* ed. John Telford (London: Epworth, 1931), 7:23-24.

2. Jim Wallis, sermon at Wesley Theological Seminary, Washington, D.C., 1992, quoted in Steven W. Manskar, "Good News to the Poor?" (Nashville: General Board of Discipleship, n.d.), 19.

3. *The Works of John Wesley,* Bicentennial Edition, vol. 2, ed. Albert C. Outler (Nashville: Abingdon, 1985), 295.

4. Theodore W. Jennings, Jr., *Good News to the Poor: John Wesley's Evangelical Economics* (Nashville: Abingdon, 1990), 53-54.

5. Ibid., 71.

6. *The Works of John Wesley,* Bicentennial Edition, vol. 19, ed. W. Reginald Ward and Richard P. Heitzenrater (Nashville: Abingdon, 1990), 46. Wesley's discomfort is evident from his journal entry. "At four in the afternoon I submitted to 'be more vile', and proclaimed in the highways the glad tidings of salvation, speaking from a little eminence in a ground adjoining to the city, to about three thousand people."

7. Donald W. Dayton, " 'Good News to the Poor': The Methodist Experience After Wesley," in *The Portion of the Poor: Good News to the Poor in the Wesleyan Tradition,* ed. M. Douglas Meeks (Nashville: Kingswood, 1995), 68.

8. Albert C. Outler, "John Wesley as Theologian—Then and Now," in *The Wesleyan Theological Heritage: Essays of Albert C. Outler,* ed. Thomas C. Oden and Leicester R. Longden (Grand Rapids: Zondervan, 1991), 62.

9. *The Works of John Wesley,* Bicentennial Edition, vol. 21, ed. W. Reginald Ward and Richard P. Heitzenrater (Nashville: Abingdon, 1992), 233.

10. Kenneth L. Carder, "Proclaiming the Gospel of Grace," in *Theology and Evangelism in the Wesleyan Heritage,* ed. James C. Logan (Nashville: Kingswood, 1994), 85.

11. Nathan O. Hatch, *The Democratization of American Christianity* (New Haven: Yale University Press, 1989), 127, 93, 89.

12. Ibid., 93.

13. Ibid., 193, 195.

14. *The Journal and Letters of Francis Asbury,* ed. Elmer T. Clark (Nashville: Abingdon, 1958), 2:687.

15. Hatch, *Democratization,* 202.

16. Outler, "Methodism in the World Christian Community," in *The Wesleyan Theological Heritage,* 247.

17. Hatch, *Democratization,* 205.

18. Daniel A. Payne, *The Semi-Centenary and the Retrospection of the African Methodist Episcopal Church* (Baltimore: Sherwood, 1866), 6, quoted in Dayton, "Good News to the Poor," 77-78.

19. B. T. Roberts, "Free Churches," *The Earnest Christian* 1 (January 1860): 6, quoted in Dayton, "Good News to the Poor," 84.

20. Carl Bangs, *Phineas F. Bresee: His Life in Methodism, the Holiness Movement, and the Church of the Nazarene* (Kansas City, Mo.: Beacon Hill, 1995), 197.

21. Roger Finke and Rodney Stark, *The Churching of America, 1776–1990: Winners and Losers in Our Religious Economy* (New Brunswick, N.J.: Rutgers University Press, 1992), 153, referring to the departure of Free Methodists.

22. John W. Gardner, *National Renewal* (joint publication of Independent Sector and the National Civic League, 1995), 1.

23. Carder, "Proclaiming the Gospel of Grace," 91.

24. Sam Roberts, *Who We Are: A Portrait of America Based on the Latest U.S. Census,* rev. ed. (New York: Times Books, 1995), 141, 145.

25. Dayton, "Good News to the Poor," 67, 70. For a somewhat different interpretation, see Jennings, *Good News to the Poor.*

26. Ibid., 86.

5. Practices Multiple Leadership

1. Mary Parker Follett, *Dynamic Administration* (New York: Harper, 1941), 286; Max DePree, *Leadership Is An Art* (1987; reprint, New York: Doubleday, 1989), 39-44; Letty M. Russell, *Growth in Partnership* (Philadelphia: Westminster, 1981), 36-37.

2. Thomas A. Langford, *Practical Divinity,* rev. ed., vol. 1, *Theology in the Wesleyan Tradition* (Nashville: Abingdon, 1998), 14.

3. Richard P. Heitzenrater, *Wesley and the People Called Methodists* (Nashville: Abingdon, 1995), 115.

4. *Autobiography of Peter Cartwright* (1856; reprint, Nashville: Abingdon, 1984), 63-64.

5. Bishop Ann B. Sherer, Stover-Ward Lecture on United Methodism, Saint Paul School of Theology, November 11, 1993.

6. Nathan O. Hatch, *The Democratization of American Christianity* (New Haven: Yale University Press, 1989), 85.

7. Jean Miller Schmidt, "Grace Sufficient for Our Day," Iliff School of Theology Opening Convocation Address, 1989–90.

8. Paul W. Chilcote, *She Offered Them Christ: The Legacy of Women Preachers in Early Methodism* (Nashville: Abingdon, 1993), 11.

9. Ibid., 22.

10. Ernst Troeltsch, *The Social Teaching of the Christian Churches* (New York: Macmillan, 1931), 2:724.

11. Albert C. Outler, "John Wesley as Theologian—Then and Now," in *The Wesleyan Theological Heritage: Essays of Albert C. Outler,* ed. Thomas C. Oden and Leicester R. Longden (Grand Rapids: Zondervan, 1991), 62.

12. Annie Dillard, *Pilgrim at Tinker Creek* (New York: Harper's Magazine Press, 1974), 34.

13. "By 1790, 11,682 blacks were counted as members of the Methodist Episcopal Church, or one-fifth of a total official membership of over 57,600. By 1800 this number had risen to 18,659, nearly one-third of the American Methodist population." Doris Elisabeth Andrews, "Popular Religion and the Revolution in the Middle Atlantic Ports: The Rise of the Methodists, 1770–1800" (Ph.D. diss., University of Pennsylvania, 1986), 218.

14. William B. McClain, *Black People in the Methodist Church: Whither Thou Goest?* (1984; reprint, Nashville: Abingdon, 1995), 40.

15. For a superb study of these preachers and other important issues of race and Methodism, see McClain's *Black People in the Methodist Church,* from which this unit draws. Also see McClain, "African American Methodists: A Remnant and a

Reminder," in *Connectionalism: Ecclesiology, Mission, and Identity,* ed. Russell E. Richey, Dennis M. Campbell, and William B. Lawrence (Nashville: Abingdon, 1997), 77-91.

16. Chilcote, *She Offered Them Christ,* 34.

17. Heitzenrater, *Wesley and the People Called Methodists,* 106.

18. Letty M. Russell, *Church in the Round: Feminist Interpretation of the Church* (Louisville: Westminster/John Knox, 1993), 56.

19. James M. Kouzes and Barry Z. Posner, *The Leadership Challenge: How to Get Extraordinary Things Done in Organizations,* 2nd ed. (San Francisco: Jossey-Bass, 1995), xx.

6. Leads from the Center and the Edge

1. Ernst Troeltsch, *The Social Teaching of the Christian Churches* (New York: Macmillan, 1931), 2:724.

2. See Kirbyjon Caldwell in Neil M. Alexander, "Breaking the Rules of Worship: Conversations with Two Pastors," *Circuit Rider* 18, no. 10 (December 1994/January 1995): 16; and James F. White, Stover-Ward Lecture on United Methodism, Saint Paul School of Theology, November 6, 1997. In drawing parallels with today, White says, "Wesley would applaud efforts of growing churches to adapt worship to reach people but not be as pleased with the abandonment of regard for Christian liturgical traditions found in some of these churches."

3. Robert C. Neville, "Truth and Tradition," in *Truth and Tradition: A Conversation About the Future of United Methodist Theological Education,* ed. Neal F. Fisher (Nashville: Abingdon, 1995), 48. Wesley's attitude toward tradition relative to evangelization was "that Christian traditions are strong enough to be put at risk for the sake of reaching new people with the gospel."

4. Lyman Beecher, *An Address to the Charitable Society for the Education of Indigent Pious Young Men for the Ministry of the Gospel* (New Haven, 1814), 7, quoted in Nathan O. Hatch, *The Democratization of American Christianity* (New Haven: Yale University Press, 1989), 18.

5. Hatch, *Democratization,* 46.

6. *The Journal and Letters of Francis Asbury,* ed. J. Manning Potts (Nashville: Abingdon, 1958), 3:164, quoted in Hatch, *Democratization,* 89; Hatch, *Democratization,* 85; Francis Asbury, *The Arminian Magazine* 7 (1784): 681, quoted in Hatch, *Democratization,* 85.

7. William Warren Sweet, *Religion on the American Frontier, 1783–1840,* vol. 4, *The Methodists* (Chicago: University of Chicago Press, 1946), 3, 29.

8. *The Works of the Rev. John Wesley, A.M.,* ed. Thomas Jackson, 3rd ed. (London: John Mason, 1831), 7:290, quoted in Donald W. Dayton, " 'Good News to the Poor': The Methodist Experience After Wesley," in *The Portion of the Poor: Good News to the Poor in the Wesleyan Tradition,* ed. M. Douglas Meeks (Nashville: Kingswood, 1995), 70.

9. Peter Cartwright, *Autobiography of Peter Cartwright* (1856; reprint, Nashville: Abingdon, 1984), 64.

10. William Warren Sweet, *Methodism in American History* (New York: Methodist Book Concern, 1933, 337-38, quoted in Roger Finke and Rodney Stark, *The Churching of America, 1776–1990: Winners and Losers in Our Religious Economy* (New Brunswick, N.J.: Rutgers University Press, 1992), 160.

11. Quoted in Jean Miller Schmidt, "Reexamining the Public/Private Split: Reforming the Continent and Spreading Scriptural Holiness," in *Perspectives on*

American Methodism: Interpretive Essays, ed. Russell E. Richey, Kenneth E. Rowe, and Jean Miller Schmidt (Nashville: Kingswood, 1993), 233.

12. George R. Crooks, *The Life of Bishop Matthew Simpson* (New York: Harper and Bros., 1891), 395ff.

13. Clarence True Wilson, *Matthew Simpson: Patriot, Preacher, and Prophet* (New York: Methodist Book Concern, 1929), 75.

14. Crooks, *Bishop Matthew Simpson,* 403.

15. Ibid., 507.

16. Robert Wuthnow, *The Restructuring of American Religion: Society and Faith Since World War II* (Princeton: Princeton University Press, 1988); Martin Marty, foreword to *Understanding Church Growth and Decline, 1950–1978,* ed. Dean R. Hoge and David A. Roozen (New York: Pilgrim, 1979), 10; Harvey Cox, *Harvard Business Review* 72, no. 3 (May-June 1994): 144.

17. Warren Carter, "For the Little Ones: Matthew from and on the Margins," Inaugural Lecture, Lindsey P. Pherigo Chair in New Testament, Saint Paul School of Theology, April 11, 1996.

18. William R. Hutchison, ed., *Between the Times: The Travail of the Protestant Establishment in America, 1900–1960* (Cambridge: Cambridge University Press, 1989), vii.

19. Walter Brueggemann, *Cadences of Home: Preaching Among Exiles* (Louisville: Westminster/John Knox, 1997). This is a careful yet accessible description of the contemporary context of American mainline churches in light of scriptural resources.

20. C. Kirk Hadaway and David A. Roozen, *Rerouting the Protestant Mainstream* (Nashville: Abingdon, 1995), 112.

21. Richard Bondi, *Leading God's People: Ethics for the Practice of Ministry* (Nashville: Abingdon, 1989), 17, 71; Rosita deAnn Mathews, "Using Power from the Periphery," in Emilie M. Townes, ed., *A Troubling in My Soul: Womanist Perspectives on Evil and Suffering* (Maryknoll, N.Y.: Orbis, 1993), 105.

22. Bondi, *Leading God's People,* 17.

23. Ibid., 71.

24. Carter, "For the Little Ones."

25. Gerald Early, "Martin Luther King and the Middle Way," *Christian Century* 113, no. 25 (August 28-September 4, 1996): 816-20; "In short, King served as the center between black and white and as the center between black radicalism and black conservatism," 817.

26. Dayton, "Good News to the Poor," 71.

27. L. Gregory Jones, "Theology for the Third Millennium," *Duke Divinity News and Views* 13, no. 2 (Winter 1998): 5.

28. Christine Leigh Heyrman, *Southern Cross: The Beginnings of the Bible Belt* (New York: Knopf, 1997). Quotation is from an interview with the author, "Before the Bible Belt," by Jerome Weeks, *Dallas Morning News,* 21 June 1997.

7. Lives in a Tension

1. Richard P. Heitzenrater, *Mirror and Memory: Reflections on Early Methodist History* (Nashville: Kingswood, 1989), 56; *Wesley and the People Called Methodists* (Nashville: Abingdon, 1995), 321.

2. Clarence True Wilson, *Matthew Simpson: Patriot, Preacher, Prophet* (New York: Methodist Book Concern, 1929), 39.

3. Ralph Ellison, *Invisible Man* (New York: Modern Library, 1994), 570.

4. Robert Bellah, Slater-Willson Lecture, Saint Paul School of Theology, 1976.

5. Albert C. Outler, "John Wesley as Theologian—Then and Now," in *The Wesleyan Theological Heritage: Essays of Albert C. Outler,* ed. Thomas C. Oden and Leicester R. Longden (Grand Rapids: Zondervan, 1991), 58.

6. Albert C. Outler, "A New Future for Wesley Studies: An Agenda for 'Phase III,' " in *The Wesleyan Theological Heritage,* 135-36.

7. Heitzenrater, *Mirror and Memory,* 56.

8. Ibid.

9. Mary Elizabeth Mullino Moore, "Poverty, Human Depravity, and Prevenient Grace," *Quarterly Review* 16, no. 4 (Winter 1996–1997): 356-57.

10. Albert C. Outler, *John Wesley's Sermons: An Introduction* (Nashville: Abingdon, 1991), 22, quoting Josiah Tucker, *A Brief History of the Principles of Methodism* (Oxford, 1742), 39.

11. James C. Logan, "The Evangelical Imperative: A Wesleyan Perspective," in *Theology and Evangelism in the Wesleyan Heritage* (Nashville: Kingswood, 1994), 19.

12. Mary Elizabeth Mullino Moore, "To Search and to Witness: Theological Agenda of Georgia Harkness," *Quarterly Review* 13, no. 3 (1993): 16.

13. Georgia Harkness, *Understanding the Christian Faith* (New York: Abingdon-Cokesbury, 1947), 49, quoted in Rosemary Skinner Keller, *Georgia Harkness: For Such a Time as This* (Nashville: Abingdon, 1992), 247.

14. Mary Parker Follett, *Creative Experience* (New York: Longmans, Green and Company, 1924), 156, 162, 163.

15. Ibid., 174.

16. Ibid., 163.

17. Letty M. Russell, *Growth in Partnership* (Philadelphia: Westminster, 1981), 34-35.

18. Outler, "John Wesley as Theologian," 58.

19. James C. Collins and Jerry I. Porras, *Built to Last: Successful Habits of Visionary Companies* (New York: Harper Business, 1994), 43-44. A helpful application of this approach to religious leadership is H. Newton Malony, *Living with Paradox: Religious Leadership and the Genius of Double Vision* (San Francisco: Jossey-Bass, 1998).

20. Barbara Brown Taylor, Yale Divinity School *Reflections* (Summer-Fall, 1993): 11.

8. Seeks to Include

1. Mary Parker Follett, *The New State* (New York: Longmans, Green and Company, 1923), 36-37.

2. Mary Parker Follett, *Creative Experience* (New York: Longmans, Green and Company, 1924), 174.

3. Georgia Harkness, *Understanding the Christian Faith* (New York: Abingdon-Cokesbury, 1947), 49, quoted in Rosemary Skinner Keller, *Georgia Harkness: For Such a Time as This* (Nashville: Abingdon, 1992), 247.

4. Mary Elizabeth Mullino Moore, "Poverty, Human Depravity, and Prevenient Grace," *Quarterly Review* 16, no. 4 (Winter 1996–97): 357.

5. Albert C. Outler, "A New Future for Wesley Studies: An Agenda for 'Phase III,' " in *The Wesleyan Theological Heritage: Essays of Albert C. Outler,* ed. Thomas C. Oden and Leicester R. Longden (Grand Rapids: Zondervan, 1991), 135-36.

6. "Congregations in the Midst of Change: An Interview with Nancy Ammerman," *Christian Century* 114, no. 2 (15 January 1997): 50.

7. Kenneth L. Carder, *Living Our Beliefs: The United Methodist Way* (Nashville: Discipleship Resources, 1996), 4.

8. *The Works of John Wesley,* Bicentennial Edition, vol. 7, ed. Franz Hildebrandt (Nashville: Abingdon, 1989), 117, quoted in Albert C. Outler, *John Wesley's Sermons: An Introduction* (Nashville: Abingdon, 1991), 28.

9. Nathan O. Hatch, "The Puzzle of American Methodism," in *American Church History: A Reader,* ed. Henry Warner Bowden and P. C. Kemeney (Nashville: Abingdon, 1998), 284.

10. *Love Letters from Cell 92: The Correspondence Between Dietrich Bonhoeffer and Maria von Wedemeyer 1943–1945,* ed. Ruth-Alice von Bismarck and Ulrich Kabitz, trans. John Brownjohn (Nashville: Abingdon, 1992), 229.

11. David A. Roozen and C. Kirk Hadaway, "Individuals and the Church Choice," in *Church and Denominational Growth,* ed. David A. Roozen and C. Kirk Hadaway (Nashville: Abingdon, 1995), 249.

12. Joel Kotkin and Yoriko Kishimoto, *The Third Century: America's Resurgence in the Asian Era* (New York: Crown, 1988), 1-2.

13. Steven A. Holmes, "Hispanics Dominate Shift in U.S. Population," *International Herald Tribune,* 15 March 1996, 1, 10. "More Than a Question of Black and White," *American Demographics,* Black Americans Reprint Package (1994), 3, 5.

14. Holmes, "Hispanics Dominate Shift," 1, 10.

15. Robert Samuelson, "How Immigration Blurs U.S. Snapshot," *Richmond Times-Dispatch,* 5 August 1996, A9.

16. Kotkin and Kishimoto, *The Third Century,* 2.

17. Sam Roberts, *Who We Are: A Portrait of America Based on the Latest Census,* rev. ed. (New York: Times Books, 1995), 63.

18. Joel Kotkin, "In America, the Middle Class Heads for the Hills," *International Herald Tribune,* 14 March 1996.

19. Holmes, "Hispanics Dominate Shift in U.S. Population," 10.

20. C. Kirk Hadaway, "Church Growth in North America: The Character of a Religious Marketplace," in *Church and Denominational Growth,* 351.

21. Follett, *Creative Experience,* 162.

22. "A Conversation with Tex Sample and Emilie Townes," *Alive Now* 25, no. 5 (September/October 1995): 20.

23. Letty M. Russell, *Growth in Partnership* (Philadelphia: Westminster, 1981), 34-35.

24. Frederick Buechner, *Telling Secrets* (San Francisco: Harper, 1991), 58-59.

25. Carl S. Dudley, "Pluralism as an Ism," *Christian Century* 110, no. 30 (27 October 1993): 1041.

9. Makes "Connection" Happen

1. Dennis M. Campbell, "A Conversation with Dennis Campbell and Russell Richey," *Initiatives in Religion* (Lilly Endowment, Inc.) 4, no. 1 (Winter 1995): 4. "Reconnecting Methodism: Our Theological Task," *Circuit Rider* 20, no. 9 (November 1996): 6.

2. Campbell, "Reconnecting Methodism," 7.

3. Russell E. Richey, "Twins: The Local Church and Denominational Bureaucracy," *Leadership Letters* (Duke Divinity School) 1, no. 5 (30 July 1995).

4. Richey, "Twins," 2.

5. Ibid.

6. Russell E. Richey, *The Methodist Conference in America: A History* (Nashville: Kingswood, 1996), 182; "Vital Connectionalism," *Circuit Rider* 20, no. 9 (November 1996): 17.

7. Russell E. Richey, "Vital Connectionalism," 17-19. For a more extensive elaboration on these principles and other important dimensions of connectionalism, see *Connectionalism: Ecclesiology, Mission, and Identity,* ed. Russell E. Richey, Dennis M. Campbell, and William B. Lawrence (Nashville: Abingdon, 1997), especially the introduction by Richey.

8. Richey, "Twins," 6.

9. Campbell, "Reconnecting Methodism," 7.

10. A. Gregory Schneider, *The Way of the Cross Leads Home: A Domestication of American Methodism* (Bloomington: Indiana University Press, 1993), xiii.

11. Rosabeth Moss Kanter, "Ourselves Versus Ourselves," *Harvard Business Review* 70, no. 3 (May-June 1992): 10.

12. Ibid.

13. Ibid.

14. See Richard P. Heitzenrater, "Connectionalism and Itinerancy: Wesleyan Principles and Practice," in *Connectionalism: Ecclesiology, Mission, and Identity,* 23-38. The quotation is from page 35.

15. Kanter, "Ourselves," 10.

10. Knows God

1. *The Works of John Wesley,* Bicentennial Edition, vol. 1, ed. Albert C. Outler (Nashville: Abingdon, 1984), 691.

2. Quoted in James I. Packer, introduction to *The Reformed Pastor* by Richard Baxter (1656; 5th abridged edition, 1862; reprint, Edinburgh: Banner of Truth Trust, 1974), 9, 15.

3. Baxter, *Reformed Pastor,* 14, 53, 54; *The Letters of the Rev. John Wesley, A.M.,* ed. John Telford (London: Epworth, 1931), 1:301.

4. *The Works of John Wesley,* Bicentennial Ed., vol. 1, 408, 413.

5. Will D. Campbell, *Forty Acres and a Goat* (San Francisco: Harper and Row, 1988), 154-59.

6. *The Lutheran Book of Worship* (Minneapolis: Augsburg, 1978), 137.

7. Langston Hughes, "Let America Be America Again," *The Poetry of the Negro, 1746–1970,* ed. Langston Hughes and Arna Bontemps (New York: Doubleday, 1970), 195.

8. Letty M. Russell, *Human Liberation in a Feminist Perspective: A Theology* (Philadelphia: Westminster, 1974), 143.

9. *John Wesley's Commentary on the Bible,* ed. G. Roger Schoenhals (Grand Rapids: Zondervan, 1990), 507.

10. Deborah Baldwin, "The Doctor Is In," *Common Cause* 68 (May/June 1988): 28.

11. William McKinney, *Bulletin* (Pacific School of Religion) 75, no. 1 (Fall 1996).

12. *The Lutheran Book of Worship,* 137.

11. Proclaims Christ

1. John Wesley, "The Law Established Through Faith, Discourse II," in *The Works of John Wesley,* Bicentennial Edition, vol. 2, ed. Albert C. Outler (Nashville: Abingdon, 1985), 37.

2. It is reported that this was Hoosier's response when someone inquired about

his illiteracy. Quoted in William B. McClain, *Black People in the Methodist Church: Whither Thou Goest?* (1984; reprint, Nashville: Abingdon, 1995), 42.

3. *The Works of the Rev. John Wesley, A.M.,* ed. Thomas Jackson, 3rd ed. (London: John Mason, 1831), 8:310.

4. Ibid.

5. Ibid., 13:418.

6. William McKinney, *Bulletin* (Pacific School of Religion) 75, no. 1 (Fall 1996).

7. Ibid.

8. C. K. Barrett, *A Commentary on the First Epistle to the Corinthians* (New York: Harper & Row, 1968), 95.

9. Thomas G. Long, "Preaching About Hope," lecture at Central Baptist Theological Seminary, 1996.

10. Peter Schmiechen, *Christ the Reconciler: A Theology for Opposites, Differences, and Enemies* (Grand Rapids: Eerdmans, 1996), 89.

11. Albert C. Outler, *John Wesley's Sermons: An Introduction* (Nashville: Abingdon, 1991), 104.

12. James C. Logan, "The Evangelical Imperative: A Wesleyan Perspective," in *Theology and Evangelism in the Wesleyan Heritage* (Nashville: Kingswood, 1994), 17.

13. Walter Brueggemann, *Biblical Perspectives on Evangelism: Living in a Three-Storied Universe* (Nashville: Abingdon, 1993), 90.

14. Ibid., 14.

15. Ibid., 15.

16. Georgia Harkness, *The Gospel and Our World* (New York: Abingdon, 1949), 24, quoted in Rosemary Skinner Keller, *Georgia Harkness: For Such a Time as This* (Nashville: Abingdon, 1992), 246.

17. Harkness, *Gospel and Our World,* 14-15, quoted in Keller, *Georgia Harkness,* 246.

18. Leander E. Keck, *The Church Confident* (Nashville: Abingdon, 1993), 117.

19. McClain, *Black People in the Methodist Church,* 51-54.

12. Seeks Justice

1. *The Works of the Rev. John Wesley, A.M.,* ed. Thomas Jackson, 3rd ed. (London: John Mason, 1831), 14:321.

2. Kenneth E. Boulding, *Religious Perspectives of College Teaching in Economics* (New Haven: Edward W. Hazen Foundation, n.d.), 18, quoted in S. Paul Schilling, *Methodism and Society in Theological Perspective* (Nashville: Abingdon, 1960), 64. Wilberforce quoted in Albert C. Outler, *Willson Lectures* (Washington, D.C.: Wesley Theological Seminary, 1973), 15.

3. William B. McClain, *Black People in the Methodist Church: Whither Thou Goest?* (1984; reprint, Nashville: Abingdon, 1995), 4-5.

4. *Extracts of the Journals of the Late Rev. Thomas Coke* (Dublin: Methodist Book-Room, 1816), 74, quoted in Donald E. Messer, "Where Do We Go from Here?" in *Send Me? The Itineracy in Crisis* (Nashville: Abingdon, 1991), 160; McClain, *Black People in the Methodist Church,* 56.

5. See Donald W. Dayton, *Discovering an Evangelical Heritage* (New York: Harper & Row, 1976), 73-77.

6. James S. Thomas, *Methodism's Racial Dilemma: The Story of the Central Jurisdiction* (Nashville: Abingdon, 1992), 43.

7. Donald W. Dayton, " 'Good News to the Poor': The Methodist Experience

After Wesley," in *The Portion of the Poor: Good News to the Poor in the Wesleyan Tradition,* ed. M. Douglas Meeks (Nashville: Kingswood, 1995), 79.

8. Gloria Yamato, "Something About the Subject Makes It Hard to Name," in *Race, Class, and Gender: An Anthology,* 2nd ed. (Belmont, Calif.: Wadsworth, 1995), 72.

9. Jonathan Kozol, *Savage Inequalities: Children in America's Schools* (New York: Crown, 1991), 90, 106.

10. Martin Luther King, Jr., *Stride Toward Freedom* (New York: Harper & Row, 1958), 19.

11. Joel Kotkin, "In America, the Middle Class Heads for the Hills," *International Herald Tribune,* 14 March 1996.

12. Ibid.

13. Joel Kotkin, *Tribes: How Race, Religion, and Global Identity Determine Success in the New Global Economy* (New York: Random House, 1993), 3.

14. Ibid.

15. Ibid., 3-4.

16. Ibid., 4.

17. Richard P. Heitzenrater, *Wesley and the People Called Methodists* (Nashville: Abingdon, 1995), 321.

18. Reinhold Niebuhr, "Theology and Political Thought in the Western World," in *Faith and Politics,* ed. Ronald Stone (New York: George Braziller, 1968), 55, quoted in Robin W. Lovin, *Reinhold Niebuhr and Christian Realism* (Cambridge: Cambridge University Press, 1995), 48; Rebecca S. Chopp, *Saving Work* (Louisville: Westminster/John Knox, 1995), 64.

19. Claude H. Thompson, "Reflections on Dallas," *Mississippi United Methodist Advocate,* 6 January 1971, 5.

Conclusion

1. Richard P. Heitzenrater, *Wesley and the People Called Methodists* (Nashville: Abingdon, 1995), 321.

2. *The Letters of the Rev. John Wesley, A.M.,* ed. John Telford (London: Epworth, 1931), 7:175-76, quoted in Paul W. Chilcote, *She Offered Them Christ: The Legacy of Women Preachers in Early Methodism* (Nashville: Abingdon, 1993), 107.